Leading
like
Francis

More Praise for *Leading Like Francis*

"Carl Koch masterfully provides stories and writings of Francis of Assisi to exemplify Robert Greenleaf's ten characteristics of a servant leader. The interplay of the thirteenth century saint with prevalent thought on leadership reflects the author's vast knowledge of servant leadership. Leaders desiring a resource for ongoing formation in servant leadership and/or Franciscan spirituality will delight in this book."

> **Ramona Miller**, OSF, Franciscan Pilgrimage leader, past president of the Franciscan Federation, and author of *In the Footsteps of Saint Clare*

"This book is a delight! Its rich mix of information, inspiration and practical guidance recognizes that everyone is called to lead -- and that leadership begins on the inside. It will draw you closer to St. Francis, inspire you with his faith and devotion, and guide you every step of the way to becoming the kind of disciple and leader who would make Jesus and Francis both smile."

> **Owen Phelps**, author of *The Catholic Vision for Leading Like Jesus* and founder of the Yeshua Catholic International Leadership Institute

"This book about servant leadership in the Franciscan tradition will affirm one's aspirations to grow and give witness to a Franciscan model of service. One's repertoire of preferred leadership behaviors is quickly enhanced in this framework of stories from scripture, Franciscan texts, and references from the insights of modern leaders."

> **Marlene Weisenbeck**, FSPA, past president of the Leadership Conference of Women Religious and the Franciscan Sisters of Perpetual Adoration

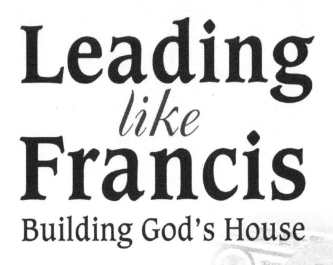

Leading *like* Francis
Building God's House

Carl Koch

NEW CITY PRESS
of the Focolare
Hyde Park, NY

Published in the United States by New City Press
202 Comforter Blvd., Hyde Park, NY 12538
www.newcitypress.com
© 2014 Carl Koch

Cover design by Leandro De Leon

Cover Photo of Work of Giotto di Bondone (1267-1337), Basilique Assise, *Legend of St. Francis, Dream of Innocent III.*

Scripture quotations are from the New Revised Standard Version Bible, copyright © 1989 National Council of the Churches of Christ in the United States of America. Used by permission. All rights reserved.

Library of Congress Control Number: 2014953243

ISBN: 978-1-56548-575-4

Printed in the United States of America

Contents

Acknowledgements 7

Introduction 9

1. Listening to God's Word Wherever Spoken 29

2. Empathy with God's People 39

3. Opening Mind and Heart 49

4. Healing the Body of Christ 59

5. Drawing All to God's Reign 71

6. Gospel Vision 79

7. Attending Now, Looking Ahead 87

8. Being the Good Steward 97

9. A Resource for Growth 105

10. Building Community 113

Epilogue 121

References and Further Reading 125

Acknowledgements

This book relies on the three-volume series *Francis of Assisi: Early Documents*, edited by Regis J. Armstrong OFM Cap, J. A. Wayne Hellmann OFM Conv, and William J. Short OFM, published by New City Press. Their authoritative edition of essential works by and about Saint Francis formed the basis of this work. To the three editors and their team of collaborators I offer my profound thanks.

In the book, all quotations from these three documents are referenced in this way:

Volume I – *The Saint*: *FS:TS*

Volume II – *The Founder*: *FS:TF*

Volume III – *The Prophet*: *FS:TP*.

While the book's focus is on the leadership of Francis of Assisi, tribute must be given to Robert Greenleaf, who was the first to formulate the concept of servant leadership. Many other authors have continued to expand his ideas, and the practice of servant leadership is reshaping organizations all over the world. My thanks and blessings go out to all who follow in the footsteps of Francis of Assisi and Robert Greenleaf.

Introduction

*W*hen Cardinal Jorge Mario Bergoglio chose the name Francis upon his election as pope, he sent an unmistakable message about the way in which he would try to lead the Church. When he chose to live in a modest apartment, to forgo many of the trappings of the papal office, washed the feet of women on Holy Thursday, and publicly went to confession to a regular priest in St. Peter's, we knew that he had fully embraced the manner of leadership of his namesake, Francis of Assisi.

The call to leadership — influencing others to follow and accomplish a shared mission — comes in many forms. Pope Francis began his journey to leadership long before becoming pope. Francis of Assisi's call to leadership came in a series of events that moved him from the privileged life of a rich kid to a way of life characterized by service, prayer, embrace of the poor, and leadership of a band of brothers — the friars minor. One of those key events occurred in San Damiano Chapel. Francis' wanderings took him by the church, which was crumbling from age and neglect. Francis entered and knelt before the crucifix. Rapt in prayer, he heard a voice from the crucifix say, "Francis, go and repair my house which, as you see, is all being destroyed" (*FA:TF* 536). Even though it took a while for Francis to fully realize what Christ meant, he embraced the call and invited others to join him.

The call to Christ-like, Franciscan leadership always invites us to "repair" or in some translations "rebuild" God's house. Christ, Francis of Assisi, and now Pope Francis teach us to lead and call us to a particular way of leading—no matter what our status or roles in life, whether parent or student, pastor or plumber, teacher or executive. We have learned to call their way of leading *servant leadership*. Central to servant leadership is building, creating, making fresh, and healing broken relationships and broken people.

When I reflect on the often subtle way Christ calls us to servant leadership, I think of two stories: one of Todd and the other of Peg.

Todd knew that something was bugging his son but, like most teens, Jack wasn't always the most communicative. As July dragged on, Jack seemed to tense up each time Todd mentioned the start of high school football practice. St. Ed's was a consistent winner. The coach was tough but fair. Getting a spot on the roster was competitive. Even so, Jack had been one of the best centers in youth football, and he was big. So Todd wondered what was going on with his son. He worried even more as he watched Jack—who usually ate his mound of spaghetti at warp speed—push his food around on his plate

"Dad, I don't want to play football," Jack blurted, catching Todd by surprise.

"You seemed pretty excited about playing last spring. What's changed?"

"I just don't want to spend all that time working out, getting banged around, and I hate having to get all worked up."

"Most of your friends will be playing. Do you think this will change things with them?"

"I don't know. I guess Randy and DJ will be ticked off. Not sure about Brandon. I think he plays because his dad did. Will you be disappointed?"

Todd knew that maybe this was the heart of the matter. He had played Division I college football and had starred at St. Ed's in high school. "I'd be disappointed if you played and didn't have your heart in it or because you didn't think you were good enough. I'd also be disappointed if you didn't develop some other interest. Have you got something else in mind to do?"

"I was thinking of playing trumpet in band."

"That'd be great. I always wanted to learn an instrument myself and never did."

Todd and his son talked some more, but soon Jack's phone jangled and he headed to his room. Todd sat at the table and smiled, glad that Jack had made a good decision. He wondered how Sara would take the news when she got off her shift at the hospital.

* * *

Peg stood at the counter at the food bank, waiting for the first client. People could come once each month for emergency food aid. For Peg, coming to a food bank to volunteer had been one of the best experiences at university. Now, as campus minister, she had worked hard to recruit students to be there with her every Friday. True to form, most of the students who committed to helping once or twice returned to help further. As April turned to May, Jenny, a faithful volunteer, turned to Peg as the last client picked up his box of food and thanked her.

"Peg, you know what I'm going to miss most about college? Coming here every Friday." Then tears coursed down her face even as she started to laugh. "Can you believe this. God, I feel dumb."

Peg hugged her. She understood.

"Thanks, Peg. Thanks for getting me to do this."

A few weeks later, Peg opened an envelope from Jenny. On a coffee-stained piece of notebook paper was this poem.

The people shuffle in
with empty bags, and
all too often vacant stares,
the odor of too many cigarettes
and not enough air.
Fridays at the food bank,
"We have green beans, corn and peas," I offer.
Then a can of fruit, maybe two,
mac and cheese, some sort of pasta,
tuna or Spam, various beans,
spaghetti sauce or diced tomatoes.
Cereal's next and soup
"Tomato? Chicken noodle?"
Peanut butter and if we're lucky crackers.
Meat next—almost out of date.
"Brats? Drumsticks? Wings?
Ground pork patties?"
Then hygiene products—
generic shampoo or toilet paper.
Finally—extras—mostly stuff donors
couldn't figure out what to do with—
artichoke hearts, enchilada mix,
piles of Twizzlers, hot sauce,
and once a jar of pectin.
The folks might mumble thanks,
or not.
Maybe a smile as we talk of
ways to cook brisket.
"Take lots of bread," I exhort.
The next one comes forward.
Good Friday communion.

Now it was Peg's turn for tears.

Todd and Peg did not think of themselves as leaders, but they certainly were. By simply listening, Todd helped his son build energy around his decision and ponder new adventures. Through Peg's invitation to volunteer, Jenny found out that she had the power to make a positive difference in people's lives.

Unfortunately, the word *leadership* has a mystique about it. Perhaps we had classmates who were referred to as *natural leaders.* Sometimes people fawned on them, and much was expected of them. We expect businesspeople, politicians, and athletes to assume a mantle of leadership. On the other hand, we less frequently associate leadership with the deep spirituality and virtues inherent in a saint like Francis, an effective pastor, or a great parent.

All leaders influence followers to accomplish goals. The worst leaders—whether pastors, parents, or executives—use coercion, manipulation, and force to make followers do things that most often primarily benefit the leader: think Stalin, Hitler, Pol Pot. The best leaders, however—the pastors, parents, and executives we admire and seek to imitate—persuade, offer good examples, and empower followers to accomplish mutually beneficial goals: think Jesus, Gandhi, Francis of Assisi, Pope Francis, Todd, and Peg.

Servant Leadership for All God's People

Jesus calls all Christians to be leaders—to influence others to love wisely and well, to live charitably, hopefully, and faithfully. In the manner of Jesus, parents lead their children by teaching them right and wrong, helping them form habits of kindness and care. Pastoral ministers lead when they invite searchers to conversation about meaning and values, when they take service trips with youth groups, or when they teach people to read the scriptures. Individuals in business show

Christ-like leadership when they manage their affairs with justice and integrity.

Leadership is a relationship between people, and we are always in relationships with others. So, we are always leaders. The key question then becomes: What sort of a leader do we wish to be? Francis of Assisi, modeling his life on Jesus, was a servant leader. If we want to walk in the footsteps of Jesus and Saint Francis, then we strive to be servant leaders too.

We know Francis of Assisi as a great saint, an example of holiness for all generations. He was also a stellar example of servant leadership, a concept that was not articulated in his time, but is important for ours. For believers, especially followers of Francis like Pope Francis, seeing him as a servant leader may help us become more effective ministers of the Gospel and People of God. Like both the Saint and the Pope, we can "rebuild" God's house by being servant leaders.

While the term *servant leadership* fits readily with Christian-Franciscan spirituality, it actually originated with the work of AT&T executive Robert Greenleaf. Many years ago, AT&T directed the young Greenleaf to figure out why some of its offices had outstanding productivity while others lagged behind. He concluded, after studying offices nationwide: The effectiveness of each branch depended on its leadership.

Based on this insight, Greenleaf set out to research the characteristics of effective leaders. After extensive study, Greenleaf formulated his description of servant leaders. In his 1977 book, *Servant Leadership: A Journey into the Nature of Legitimate Power and Greatness*, Greenleaf describes a servant leader this way:

- "The servant-leader *is* servant first…. It begins with the natural feeling that one wants to serve, to serve *first*."
- "Then conscious choice brings one to aspire to lead."

- The servant leader ensures "that other people's highest priority needs are being served."

- "The best test, and difficult to administer, is: Do those served grow as persons? Do they, *while being served*, become healthier, wiser, freer, more autonomous, more likely themselves to become servants?"

- "*And*, what is the effect on the least privileged in society; will they benefit, or, at least, not be further deprived?"

Even though Greenleaf composed this description from his research findings about effective business leaders, it resonates with what we know of Jesus from the Gospels and Francis from his story. How would Jesus lead? His answer is consistent: "If anyone wants to be first, he must be the last and the servant of all." "I am among you as one who serves." "The greatest among you must become like the youngest, and the leader like one who serves." Or consider John 13:13-17. Jesus washes the disciples' feet and says, "I have set you an example that you should do as I have done for you." Jesus and Francis served first, and their example and persuasion led their followers to be servants too.

As a Quaker Christian, Greenleaf saw these connections between his description of servant leaders and the person of Jesus. "Servant" in the Gospel passages often refers to the "suffering servant" passages in Isaiah and means "slave of the king," a close advisor and confidant of the ruler, someone with great responsibility. This servant must be a prophet and healer. So, Jesus and anyone claiming to lead in his name accept responsibility and intimacy with God and are called to be prophetic voices and healers for the community. Only service and sacrifice confer the moral authority and trust essential for leadership.

In Paul's letters, the word he most often uses for servants is *diakonos*, which means an emissary or representative of someone else. Paul called himself a servant of God, a spokesperson for Christ. So, as Christian servant leaders, followers represent Christ in word and action. They proclaim the Word of God in speech but, as importantly, in their charity or love. Ultimately, they lead others to serve as Jesus served.

In an interview on *Dateline NBC* the founder of Vanguard Investments, John Bogle, declared that servant leadership amounts to following The Golden Rule: "Do unto others as you would have them do unto you." This is the heart of Judeo-Christian ethics. And, following this key principle has accounted for much of Vanguard's success. Indeed, companies that have made servant leadership their core operating value are among those we admire because they are not only ethical companies, but successful ones too.

Christians—parents, ministers, anyone in any position—can learn many lessons from Southwest Airlines, SAS Institute, TDIndustries, and other companies committed to servant leadership. For example, from the moment a person applies for a job at Southwest, people conducting the screening are looking for the characteristics of a servant leader in the candidate. Is he or she respectful toward the receptionist (who is on the screening committee)? If someone cannot be respectful toward a receptionist, they are probably not going to treat other workers and customers well, either. Once they are hired, employees are thoroughly oriented in servant leadership. Southwest hires based on a person's attitude, rather than skills, because they can always teach specific skills. If a candidate does not have a servant leader attitude, he or she will probably not learn it.

The key factor in Southwest's success is that servant leaders guide it. So, after 9/11, Southwest Airlines was the only airline that made a profit, kept all its workers on the job, and actually adhered to its full flight schedule. The next year, while other airlines cut thousands of jobs, Southwest hired hundreds.

Servant leadership is not only affectively and ethically right, but effective in moving people and organizations toward fulfillment of their mission.

Leadership's Old Paradigm

Pastoral ministers, military officers, managers, parents, and even friends are all called to relationships of influence that move others to do things. Unfortunately, when we are not taught servant leadership, we tend to fall back on what we do know, which often is the old top-down model of leadership: command and control—a traditional military or monarchial model of leadership. Most of us may be vaguely uncomfortable with this model, but it is the model that we have seen others use.

The old model of leadership took the form of a pyramid. The commanding general, for example, was at the top, followed by colonels, then mid-level officers, then non-commissioned officers, and at the bottom was the last and largest group—the grunts. This model lives on. But the pyramid is beginning to show cracks, even in the military.

The old paradigm worked in civil society, business, and even churches when the majority of people were illiterate peasants whose lives were circumscribed by rigid boundaries of class, custom, and geography. Education and mobility have broken open rigid social systems. Many new workers in organizations have at least as good an education as their bosses. Democracy has thrived and reinforced the belief that "all persons are created equal." These two dynamics have undermined the old paradigm.

This old model of leadership also depended on a covenant with followers that said if you do a good job, work hard for an organization, you will keep your job and the organization will look after your interests. James Autry, past president of the Meredith Group and author of *The Servant Leader*, rightly claims that this old covenant is dead. Businesses hire and fire workers at will and so quickly that workers do not expect company loyalty to them, and therefore have little loyalty in return.

The increased education of laity, the recent scandals in the church, and the constant flow of information have done the same thing to the covenant that faithful members once had with their leadership in the church: If you pay, pray and obey, you will be ministered to with competence, respect, and trust, and guided on the way of salvation. The breakdown of this old covenant has led to more empty pews on Sunday, decreases in financial and personal support, and an increase in cynicism about religion.

Needed: A Fresh Model of Leading

Jesus, Francis of Assisi, and Pope Francis offer a fresh model of leadership. And, in a growing number of organizations, the old leadership paradigm is being replaced, and for good reasons. Supervisors were looking over their shoulders at the middle managers instead of helping employees do their jobs well. Many in ministry looked over their shoulders at "superiors" rather than focusing on the real needs of those to whom they ministered. Thus, the people most essential in making a business successful — the customers — were poorly served, and the folks in the pews likewise seemed of secondary importance.

The companies known for excellent service, great value, and loyal customers and employees replace the pyramid with a circle. The president empowers, supports, and resources the vice presidents, who do the same to the managers, all the way to the employees who serve the customers.

With all-volunteer armed services, the United States military has begun moving toward servant leadership in training its officers and non-commissioned officers. Speaking at Fort

Lee, Virginia, Colonel Paul Vicalvi remarked: "I believe that the trademarks of a good servant leader are competence, courage, and compassion. Those trademarks don't always come easily. Many times, they come from hard knocks in our own lives. I learned some of my lessons on what makes an effective servant leader by serving under some pretty ineffective tyrant leaders. I vowed never to be like them.... I pray that, no matter whether we wear stripes, bars, leaves, eagles, or stars, we will continually get back to the basics of true soldiering—of true servant leadership." Servant leadership has become part and parcel of training because servant leaders clearly understand that the best leaders have been servant leaders.

The Church needs rebuilding now, just as it did in Francis of Assisi's time. Pope Francis gets it. Indeed, as with every organization, the Church always needs rebirth, re-creation, rebuilding. This is indeed a time for servant leaders to come forth to reinvigorate the People of God. In Matthew 18:18-20, Jesus tells his followers: "Whatever you bind on earth will be bound in heaven, and whatever you loose on earth will be loosed in heaven.... For where two or three are gathered in my name, I am there among them." Clearly, Jesus empowers the assembled believers: women and men, old and young, poor and rich. He is urging them to be servant leaders.

Francis, Becoming a Servant Leader

The dying words of our brother Francis were, "I have done what was mine to do; may Christ teach you what is yours to do." Francis recognized that "the Most High and Glorious God" gave everyone different gifts and particular callings. Each of us is to become the image of Christ, the Servant Leader, in our own way. Knowing what servant leadership is all about can help us name our way.

Echoing many of the elements of Greenleaf's description of a servant leader, James A. Autry in *The Servant Leader* describes servant leadership in these terms:

- Leadership is "about caring for people"
- Leadership is "being a useful resource for people"
- Leadership is "being present for people"
- Leadership is "building a community at work"
- Leadership is "letting go of ego, bringing your spirit to work, being your best and most authentic self"
- Leadership is "creating a place in which people can do good work, can find meaning in their work, and can bring their spirits to work"
- Leadership is "paying attention"
- "Leadership requires love"

If the authors of the Christian Scriptures had tried to explain Jesus' way of leading, they might have used words similar to Autry's: loving, caring, resourcing, paying attention, building community. This is exactly what Jesus and Francis did, and we are called to do.

Like Pope Francis, we can learn to be servant leaders by looking at Saint Francis' growth into leadership and then by developing the characteristics of servant leadership in our own lives. The key moments in Francis' story show us how his decisions moved him more fully into servant leadership in the image of Jesus. Harvard ethicist Joseph Badaracco quite rightly calls such key points in our lives "defining moments" because "they reveal, they test, and they shape." Each defining moment in Francis' life revealed his values and beliefs, tested them in the crucible of real life, and shaped who he would become and who his followers and the Church would become.

Most of us know at least a rough outline of Francis' life. A brief retelling of his defining moments shows how God led him to become the saint and servant leader we follow today. He began by serving the genuine needs of other people and gradually led around 7,000 friars. Subsequent chapters will expand the discussion of these defining moments and ways we can develop each characteristic of a Franciscan servant leader.

True Glory: A First Choice

In 1182, Francis was born into the Bernardone family. As a successful cloth merchant, his father was a prominent member of the ascending middle class. Francis enjoyed the fruits of his father's wealth and became the leader of a band of companions. Merrymaking, singing, and partying consumed much of his time. Then, filled with dreams of glory, Francis rode to war with Perugia in 1202, where he was captured, imprisoned, and became gravely ill. Upon his release and during his long recuperation at home, life began to change for Francis. He started pondering and praying, seeking his true purpose.

In 1204, he set off to enlist in the Fourth Crusade, hoping to gain knighthood. Instead, a vision in Spoleto directed him to go home and seek God's will. Giving his armor to a poor knight, he returned to Assisi, much to the confusion of his father. We can only imagine that if he had continued to the Holy Land we might never have known of Francis of Assisi. Like a true servant leader, Francis listened to his deeper call and the action of the Holy Spirit.

Embracing the Leper: A Second Defining Moment

Once back in Assisi, Francis continued to change into a servant of the poor. He gave generously to beggars who came to his father's shop. He went off alone to meditate. And, much to his father's dismay, his interest in the cloth business diminished. Then a most dramatic decision altered everything.

Lepers were virtually the definition of the word *pariah* for people in Francis' time, just as they were in the time of Jesus. Communities like Assisi exiled lepers to remote locations and forbade them to interact with other citizens. Lepers horrified Francis, but became the source of his definitive conversion to servant leadership in Christ. One day he was riding his horse out in the countryside when he met a leper. Bonaventure describes what happened: "Remembering that he must first conquer himself if he wanted to become *a knight of Christ*, he dismounted from his horse and ran to kiss him. As the leper stretched out his hand as if to receive something, he gave him money with a kiss. Immediately mounting his horse, however, and turning all around...he could not see the leper anywhere. He began, therefore, filled with wonder and joy, to sing praises to the Lord, while proposing, because of this, to embark always on the greater" (*FA:TS*, 533-534).

From this moment, Francis embarked on a life of loving service to the poorest, most despised members of society. Servant leadership means to love, to be a resource for others so they can become "healthier, wiser, freer, and more autonomous, and more likely themselves to become servants," as Greenleaf says. Francis' example would quickly attract followers to the same life. Not only were the lepers served, but those who followed came to life in abundance also.

Rebuild My Church: Moment Three

Liberated from his fear of lepers and set on a course of service, Francis continued to meditate in the fields, praising the Creator and seeking God's will. As recounted earlier, when Francis knelt before the crucifix in San Damiano, a third key moment occurred. Christ spoke to him, "Francis, go and repair my house which, as you see, is all being destroyed" (*FA:TF* 536).

Francis went home, gathered cloth, took it to Foligno and, being an accomplished merchant, sold it for a handsome sum. Money in hand, Francis returned to San Damiano, giving the money to the poor priest for use in repairing the church and serving the downtrodden. As with all servant leaders, Francis was letting go of his ego and taking another step toward being his best, most authentic, self. Francis had taken a next step in defining his life's meaning and doing so led to his complete renunciation of his old life—the next defining moment.

Renunciation: Defining Moment Four

Naturally Francis' father flew into fury when he learned of his son's actions—to him, they were a betrayal of the family and their expectations. The elder Bernardone locked his son into a room, hoping to break him. When his father left town on business, Pica, Francis' mother, let him out of his prison. Francis immediately returned to San Damiano.

When Pietro returned and found his son gone, he rushed to San Damiano. Hauling Francis before the bishop, Pietro demanded that Francis restore what he had taken. Bonaventure takes up the story: Francis "immediately took off his clothes and gave them back to his father.... [D]runk with remarkable fervor, he even took off his trousers, and was completely stripped naked before everyone. He said to his father: "Until now I have called you father here on earth, but now I can say without reservation, 'Our Father who art in heaven,' since I have placed my treasure and all my hope in him" (*FA:TF* 538).

Francis' renunciation of his former life, and his embrace of radical poverty and service, repelled most people in Assisi. It attracted others, however, who would soon join him.

Go into the World: A Fifth Choice

In February 1208, Francis made his next step in servant leadership. Listening carefully to the reading of the Gospel during Mass, he heard Jesus sending out his disciples to preach, instructing them in the way of life that they should follow. They should carry no money, and have only one garment and no shoes or staff. Bonaventure writes that Francis "was then overwhelmed with an indescribable joy. 'This is what I want,' he said, 'this is what I desire with all my heart!' Immediately, he took off the shoes from his feet, put down his staff, denounced his wallet and money, and, satisfied with one tunic, threw away his leather belt and put on a piece of rope for a belt. He directed all his heart's desire to carry out what he had heard and to conform in every way to the rule of right living given to the apostles" (*FA:TF* 542). At this moment, Francis became the itinerant preacher and little brother that we know.

Within weeks, Francis had attracted three followers: Bernard of Quintavalle, Peter Catanio, and Giles. By the end of 1208, the band had grown by a dozen more men. As with true servant leaders, Francis—as Greenleaf describes—first began with a desire to serve. Then, his preaching and example led others to follow his life of service. Within ten years, several thousand friars had joined him.

Resignation: A Sixth Decision

Between 1208 and 1220, friars had spread throughout Europe, and Brothers had been martyred in Morocco. During these early years, Francis had approval from the Pope for his simple rule, which exhorted the Brothers to devoutly follow the Gospels.

In 1212, Clare, a young woman from another wealthy family in Assisi, left her privileged life and joined Francis and the friars at the Porziuncola, the small chapel that became the center of the community. After some weeks during which her family tried to force her back home, Clare and a small group of women settled at San Damiano. Now many women sought to follow the example of Francis and Clare in their service to God and Lady Poverty.

Francis himself traveled to Egypt and held long conversations with the Sultan, attempting to convert him. But his absence in the Middle East, combined with his reliance on the Holy Spirit instead of rules, caused the burgeoning community back in Italy to begin to stray from Francis' original vision.

In the fashion of a true servant leader, Francis judged that the community needed someone new to administer the friars and provide greater organization. Knowing he was not the right man for the job, he resigned as Minister General and called Peter Catanio to replace him. Now he was free to preach and serve, to pray and meditate. Rather than trying to hold onto his position, Francis chose the common good. He demonstrated how a servant leader gives priority to the need of the community. He put his ego aside for love.

From 1220 until his death in 1226, Francis alternated his time preaching to the People of God and, like Jesus, going off to the mountains to pray. So intense was his identification with the crucified Jesus that in 1224 he received the *stigmata*—the wounds of Jesus. In word, deeds, and even his body, Francis became the "suffering servant" leader.

Becoming Franciscan Servant Leaders

Without a desire to serve God's people—your children, poor people, coworkers, or parishioners—you would probably not be reading this book. Indeed, most people who study servant leadership are already on the path to being servant leaders. Like Francis and Pope Francis, they desire first to serve. In 1220, Francis admonished the friars: "Because I am the servant of all, I am obliged to serve all and to administer the fragrant words of my Lord to them.... We must never desire to be above others, but, instead, we must be servants and subject to every human creature for God's sake" (*FA:TS* 47-48).

A desire to serve the genuine needs of our sisters and brothers moves us inevitably to lead others to serve: to act for a common good. For many servant leaders like Francis this movement appears almost unconscious. He did not set out to found a religious community with thousands of members. But, Francis did, quite consciously, develop many of the characteristics of a servant leader, and he became a person others wished to follow.

Robert Greenleaf describes ten characteristics that servant leaders like Francis typically possess. They are: listening, empathy, awareness, healing, persuasion, foresight, conceptualization, commitment to the growth of people, stewardship, and building community.

Wonderful servant leaders do not possess these characteristics in equal measure. Some of us are better listeners than we are persuaders. Some of us have wonderful abilities to build community, but may not have developed our awareness as fully. The key to growth as a servant leader is to strive to develop these ten characteristics. And, that is what the rest of this book is about—helping us to grow in listening, empathy, and so on, using Francis as our example.

Now is the time for servant leadership in the image of Jesus and Francis to re-emerge in the Body of Christ, to be formed in all who aspire to leadership. Let all who would aspire to lead, though, first come as servants. And may servant leaders remember to "be not afraid." Jesus and Francis go before us.

1
Listening to God's Word Wherever Spoken

*E*arly in his converted life, Francis steadily prayed to discern God's will for him. Perhaps his most famous prayer is the "Prayer before the Crucifix" at San Damiano:

> Most High,
> glorious God,
> enlighten the darkness of my heart
> and give me
> true faith,
> certain hope,
> and perfect charity,
> sense and knowledge,
> Lord,
> that I may carry out
> Your holy and true command
> (*FA:ED* 40)

His faith is that if he listens, God will speak to him.

To be enlightened, Francis listens closely. Toward the end of his life, in a letter to the entire order, Francis implored his followers to listen. He pleaded, "Listen, sons of the Lord and my brothers, pay attention to my words. Incline the ear of your heart and obey the voice of the Son of God. Observe His commands with your whole heart and fulfill his counsels with a perfect mind" (*FA:ED* 116-117).

Francis practiced what he preached to the brothers. One of the central conflicts within Francis was how to balance his desire to be with God in prayer and his call to preach the Good News to the world. Bonaventure tells this story about how Francis actively sought and listened to the wisdom of others:

> He was not ashamed to ask advice in small matters from those under him, true Lesser Brother that he was, though he had learned great things from the supreme Teacher. He was accustomed to search with special eagerness in what manner, and in what way he could serve God more perfectly according to His good pleasure.
>
> As long as he lived,
> this was his highest philosophy,
> this his highest desire:
> to ask
> from the wise and the simple,
> the perfect and the imperfect,
> the young and the old,
> how he could more effectively arrive
> at the summit of perfection.

Choosing, therefore, two of the brothers, he sent them to Brother Sylvester, who...spent his time in continuous prayer on the mountain above Assisi. He was to ask God to resolve his doubt over this matter, and to send him the answer in God's name. He also asked the holy virgin Clare to consult with the purest and simplest of the virgins living under her rule, and to pray herself with the other sisters in order to seek the Lord's will in this matter. Through a miraculous revelation of the Spirit, the venerable priest and the virgin dedicated to God came to the same conclusion: that it was the divine good will that the herald of Christ should preach. (*FA:TF* 623)

From this time forward, Francis did not question his calling to preach. The friars and he went forth all over the world to spread the Word of God. But first, he listened in prayer and in relationship with a full array of advisers.

Listening as Leading

Truly effective pastoral leaders, parents, corporate executives, and friends listen well. Like Francis, they know that to love people — to meet their true needs and to help them become freer, wiser, and more autonomous — they must understand the other, and this is done first through attentive listening. Ann McGee-Cooper, a management consultant for many companies including Southwest Airlines, says: "The servant leader works to build a solid foundation of shared goals by listening deeply to understand the needs and concerns of others." Listening deeply is a skill necessary for helpful relationships of all kinds, and is expected of those in caring roles.

When Southwest Airlines entered negotiations with its pilots union, Jim Parker, the CEO, sat at the table. One of the pilots remarked, "The biggest complaint in the industry is that management doesn't listen to employees. But you can't say that at Southwest. The top guy is in the room" (*Time*, Oct. 28, 2002, 47). Servant leaders know that the success of their organization depends on the development of trusting relationships that are built on a foundation of respectful listening.

When explaining the centrality of listening in servant leadership in his book *On Becoming a Servant Leader*, Greenleaf quotes the prayer of Saint Francis, "Grant that I may seek not so much to be understood as to understand." Greenleaf knew that servant leaders must first listen. He goes on to describe listening in these ways:

- Listening "begins with attention, both the outward manifestation and the inward alertness"
- The good listener will "retain what is expressed and refrain from piecemeal value judgments"
- Good listeners try "to hear everything that is said, not just what the listener expects or wants to hear"
- Good listening "communicates something that is universally good: attentiveness"
- Such listening "saves time in the process of communicating, and it gives the listener a better grasp of what other people" are saying, and "how they feel about what they are saying"

For many servant leaders—whether a parent, teacher, pastor, executive, or social worker—listening is a quality of character that must be learned and practiced consciously.

In our desire to lead as Christ and Francis did, we can become better listeners. The epistle attributed to James admonishes, "My beloved, let everyone be quick to listen, slow to speak" (1:19). This is sound advice for anyone in leadership, whether Franciscan or CEO, pastoral associate or salesperson, parent or professor.

Becoming a Franciscan Listener

- When facilitating workshops on servant leadership, I often share Robert Greenleaf's suggestion about listening: "Every week, set aside an hour to listen to somebody who might have something to say that will be of interest. It should be conscious practice in which all of the impulses to argue, inform, judge, and 'straighten out' the other person are denied. Every response should be calculated to reflect interest, understanding, seeking for more knowledge."

I then recommended that each workshop participant pick one person to listen to for one month, and this person should be someone that they previously found hard to listen to. No matter what they were doing, they were to stop any activity other than listening to the person. Some kept a brief log of the experience in which they recorded one or two reflections about their experience each day.

The learning from this activity was often startling. One mother of five children decided to focus on her middle child, who regularly interrupted whatever she was doing to annoyingly talk—to her mind—on and on. For a month, whenever the young boy came to talk, she ceased all activity and listened. Through copious tears she reported to her group that she rediscovered what a wonderful child he was. And, she added, his interruptions "took only a couple of minutes when I really listened. I understood sadly that as a middle child he just needed my undivided attention for a few minutes. If I just listened totally, he was a happy kid."

Listening is not only a respectful way to treat other people, it is an efficient way to relate to them. Good listening saves all of us time because it improves our relationships, creating harmony and understanding instead of friction.

- Kent Keith, former head of the Greenleaf Institute for Servant Leadership, recommends these listening practices, which can be helpful to pastors, catechists, and all of us who work with other people: Servant leaders listen "in as many ways as possible.... They observe what people are doing.... They conduct informal interviews, formal interviews, surveys, discussion groups, and focus groups. They use suggestions boxes. They do marketing studies and needs assessments. They are always asking, listening, watching, and thinking about what they learn." By listening, servant leaders are able to identify the needs of their colleagues and customers. That puts them in a good position to *meet* those needs. When they do, their organizations are successful—their colleagues are able to perform at a high level, and they have happy customers, clients, patients, members, students, or citizens.

If you work in any type of organization, ponder and jot down how you use the methods of listening that Keith mentions. Then do some brainstorming about how you might include more ways of listening. Ask yourself these questions:

○ When decisions need to be made, do I seek a wide range of views, inclusive of as many people as possible?

○ At meetings or even informal gatherings, do I ask for input from everyone when discussing issues? If we have an agenda, do I seek items from everyone?

○ What systematic methods do I use to listen to my parishioners? Students? Customers? Family members? Coworkers?

• In all of his writings, Francis constantly interjected passages from the Bible. His first rule presented to Pope Innocent III basically came down to "follow the teaching and footprints of our Lord Jesus Christ" (*FA:TS* 64). When he had a discernment to make, Francis listened to the counsel of others, but also concentrated on Gospel teachings. Listening to God's Word enlightens and enlivens our ministry and all of our relationships.

Francis did not outline a method of listening to the Gospels—that was not his style. For centuries, however, the practice of *lectio divina* or holy study has provided us with one way of listening to God's Word.

Here are directions for the practice of *lectio divina*—listening to God's Word. Note that *lectio* may be done alone or with a community, so those directions are included:

o Select a brief passage from the Bible, Francis' writings, or some other inspirational text. You might, for example, use one of the quotations from Francis or the story about him in this chapter.

o Center and relax in silence for some time. Take some deep breaths and invite the Holy Spirit to join you.

o Slowly read the passage; let your heart work through it, tasting words or phrases that seem to invite special attention. [In a group, someone reads the passage aloud slowly and clearly.]

o Repeat over and over again one line that seems to be especially important for you; let its import become clear to you. [Group: Invite participants to share the line that caught their attention.]

o Read the passage again—slowly, attentively. [Group: Read it aloud again.]

o Ponder the reading with this question in mind: How does this reading touch my life at this particular time? [Group: Ask participants to share their reflections on the question.]

o Slowly read the passage once again.

o In your mind and heart, formulate a one-word or short-phrase response to the reading. Recite a word or phrase response to the reading in harmony with your breathing. [Group: Participants share their responses.]

o End with a quiet period, a prayer, or just thoughts of thankfulness.

o Here is a passage for *lectio* from Sirach 6:33-37:

If you love to listen you will gain knowledge,
and if you pay attention you will become wise.
Stand in the company of the elders.

Who is wise? Attach yourself to such a one.
Be ready to listen to every godly discourse,
and let no wise proverb escape you.
If you see an intelligent person,
rise early to visit him;
let your foot wear out his doorstep.
Reflect on the statutes of the Holy One,
and meditate at all times
on God's commandments.
It is God who will give insight to your mind,
and your desire for wisdom will be granted.

• Finally, part of pastoral leadership, parenting, and living fully means making enlightened decisions. And, again, a key to good decision-making is listening: to the facts, to wisdom from God and other people, to our hearts and values. This LISTEN model offers a guide for discernment. Like Francis, formulate a question for which you need an answer or simply more perspective. Then move the question through the LISTEN process and see what new light is shed on the issue.

  ○ Look for the facts: What is the real situation? Who is involved? What are the elements or dynamics of the dilemma? How has the situation arisen?

  ○ Imagine possibilities: Consider creative approaches, options in line with your beliefs and convictions. Then imagine the consequences of various courses of action.

  ○ Seek insights beyond your own: Look for guidance from the Bible, tradition, family, moral principles, and wisdom figures. Listen to what they have to tell you.

  ○ Turn inward: Examine your feelings, insights from experience, motives, and values.

- ° Expect God's help: God is with you, so ask for God's guidance. It will be given.
- ° Name your decision and act.

Final Reflection

Renowned psychiatrist Karl Menninger remarked, "Listening is a magnetic and strange thing, a creative force. The friends who listen to us are the ones we move toward. When we are listened to, it creates us, makes us unfold and expand." Servant leaders are often the people we move toward—people like Jesus, Francis, and Pope Francis. They listen with the "ear of their heart," as Francis says.

So, in growing toward servant leadership, we frequently offer Francis' prayer: "Most High, glorious God, enlighten the darkness of my heart and give me true faith, certain hope, and perfect charity, sense and knowledge, Lord, that I may carry out Your holy and true command" (*FA:TS* 40).

2

Empathy with God's People

*I*n Harper Lee's *To Kill a Mockingbird*, Atticus Finch wisely tells his daughter Scout: "You can never understand someone unless you understand their point-of-view, climb in that person's skin or stand and walk in that person's shoes." This is a perfect description of empathy, the next characteristic that Francis teaches is key to ministering, administering, or parenting. It is a quality he manifested abundantly.

In *The Major Legend of Saint Francis*, Bonaventure relates this story of Francis' great empathy:

> One night, when one of the brothers was tormented with hunger because of his excessive fasting, he was unable to get any rest. The pious shepherd understood the danger threatening his sheep, called the brother, put some bread before him, and, to take away his embarrassment, he started eating first and gently invited him to eat. The brother put aside his embarrassment, took the food, overjoyed that, through the discerning condescension of his shepherd, he had both avoided harm to his body, and received an edifying example of no small proportion. (*FA:TF* 565)

Bonaventure uses the words *understood* and *discerning condescension*, but he could have easily called Francis' approach *empathy*. Putting himself in the situation of the devout friar, Francis took an approach that saved him.

Francis' empathy also comes into focus in this story:

> A certain brother, devoted to God and to Christ's servant, frequently turned over in his heart the idea: whomever the holy man embraced with intimate affection would be worthy of divine favor. Whomever he excluded, on the other hand, he would not regard among God's chosen ones. He was obsessed by the repeated pressure of this thought and intensely longed for the intimacy of the man of God, but never revealed the secret of his heart to anyone. The devoted father called him and spoke gently to him in this way: "Let no thought disturb you, my son, because, holding you dearest among those very dear to me, I gladly lavish upon you my intimacy and love." The brother was amazed at this and became even more devoted. Not only did he grow in his love of the holy man, but, through the grace of the Holy Spirit, he was also filled with still greater gifts. (*FA:TF* 617-618)

By paying attention to this anxious friar and reverencing his fears, Francis was able to respond in such a loving and wise way that the friar became filled with still greater gifts. And this is what servant leaders do. Empathy is not so much about being "nice," but more about serving the genuine needs of people once we understand them by standing in their shoes.

The centrality of empathy in pastoral ministry, parenting, teaching, or any other helping profession may seem obvious. Empathy's role in effective leadership is becoming more profoundly understood even in business, educational institutions, and perhaps not surprisingly in the military. Col. Eric Kail, field artillery officer and teacher of military leadership at West Point, declared:

> Perhaps the most pervasive axiom on the topic of leadership is that *leadership is all about people.* This simple statement reveals two critical principles of effective leadership. First,

leadership is more than accomplishing a goal or mission. Second, seeing as the word "people" is plural, the focus of who benefits from leadership should be on the followers, not the leader.

These truths, in turn, rest upon empathy, one's capacity to comprehend or experience the emotions of another. Followers view leaders in terms of the personal impact made on the followers' lives. Unfortunately, many leaders spend all their energy trying to impress others when they could be truly impressive by learning more about those whom they lead.

Francis knew this instinctively. He sought first to understand, not to be understood.

Empathy is not only at the heart of servant leadership, it is, indeed, at the heart of all moral growth. After all, the two great commandments of the Bible—and of the world religions—are to love God and to love other people. Loving others requires empathy. We can hardly foster the good of others unless we understand them, unless we can stand in their shoes and see the world, even partially, from their point of view. Without empathy, we would be amoral. I learned this truth through a sad experience that still haunts me.

Almost forty years ago, I was teaching at a Catholic high school in the Midwest. As head of the English department, I usually assigned myself the freshmen English class that was filled with the kids who had scored lowest on the entrance exam. One of the students puzzled me. Paul (not his real name) was always polite and obedient, but he seldom had his homework and often could barely stay awake. When I asked him how I could help, he was evasive. Calling his parents proved frustrating and unhelpful. When Paul was absent for two days in a row, I checked with the assistant principal. The news shocked all of us. Paul had been arrested for over thirty counts of breaking and entering and multiple charges of "joyriding"—stealing cars, riding around, and returning them.

When the police asked Paul about all the stolen goods in his basement room, he said that he didn't know how they got there. He appeared totally confused that anything was wrong. The wise juvenile judge sent Paul to a renowned child psychologist for an evaluation. The report concluded that Paul had no sense of right or wrong; he was amoral. I will never forget the psychologist's sad conclusion: "Paul has no understanding of the effect that his actions have on others. He is devoid of empathy. I am afraid that without any sense of right or wrong and the bad consequences of his behavior on others he is likely to spend much of his life in trouble and in jail." Sadly, his prophesy turned out to be correct. No empathy; no morality. And no love.

Servant leaders love others; that is, they foster the good of other people. This demands empathy, the ability to put aside my ego and walk in someone else's shoes. So naturally, the New Testament urges us to grow in the practice of empathy. Paul writes to the Romans: "Rejoice with those who rejoice, weep with those who weep. Live in harmony with one another; do not be haughty, but associate with the lowly; do not claim to be wiser than you are" (12:15-16). And Francis urged the friars to do likewise.

In his "Earlier Rule," Francis says that the friars "must rejoice when they live among people considered of little value and looked down upon, among the poor and the powerless, the sick and the lepers, and the beggars by the wayside." He reminds his brothers that Jesus "was poor and a stranger and lived on alms" (*FA:TS* 70). Citing the Golden Rule, Francis adds, "Let them behave among themselves according to what the Lord says: Do to others what you would have them do to you" (*FA:TS* 66). Further, Francis even directed the friars to join the farmers and poor folk who worked with their hands—to not only help them, but to understand them too:

"I worked with my hands...and I earnestly desire all brothers to give themselves to honest work" (*FA:TS* 125). The rule of Francis and the life of the friars were a school of empathy.

Liberation theologian Leonardo Boff points to Francis' recreation of the crib at Greccio as his way of entering more totally into the Incarnation. Through recreating the scene in the manger, Francis said, "I desire to celebrate the memory of the child who was born in Bethlehem, and I want to contemplate in some way with my eyes what he suffered in his infant weakness, how he lay in the manger, and how he was placed between the ox and the ass." By re-enacting the birth of Jesus, Francis could empathize with the child Jesus, Mary, Joseph, and shepherds. He encouraged the practice because he wanted his followers to truly come to know Christ.

Learning Franciscan Empathy

- Francis understood that we can grow in empathy, but for many of us it takes conscious effort. The following suggestions might help us all learn empathy:

  - Empathy begins with what Francis called "listening with the ear of our heart." Listen—truly listen to people. Listen with your ears, eyes, and heart.

  - Next, we should attend to body language and tone of voice, and context of the situation.

  - Avoid interrupting and giving advice; simply attend to what the other person is saying.

  - Refer to people by the name they prefer.

  - Be fully present to people, which means turning away from your computer or cell phone.

  - Smile a lot. Smiling releases endorphins, thus helping your attitude. People tend to smile in return.

- ○ Gently encourage people to speak in gatherings or meetings. Try never to insist, but to invite. Offer an attentive nod, so people know you are listening.

- ○ Finally, pay attention to what people are doing and focus on when they do the right things. Make your recognition genuine and specific: "You are an asset to this team because"; "I would have missed this if you hadn't picked it up."

Empathy is a discipline: that is, a quality we learn as disciples of a wise teacher. Francis can teach us empathy if we open our hearts to learn.

- We truly see what people believe about others in how they treat people who are not useful to them. Ponder this notion, and bring to mind people in your life who are "not useful" to you. Reflect upon your treatment of them and how you might increase your empathy for each one.

- Look for occasions to recognize a child's, a parishioner's, a coworker's good performance. Instead of offering only verbal recognition, ask if you can spend an hour or so learning how they do a particular task so well. Learn from them.

- James Autry in *The Servant Leader* declares: "I do have a piece of advice — quick but not so easy — and I offer it to new managers, to would-be servant leaders, and even to parents: When you are tempted to tell someone what to do, instead ask the question, 'What do you think you should do now?' Or in an organizational setting, 'What do you think we should do?' This is the only quick tip I have, but believe me, it can work magic. Remember, when tempted to tell, ask instead." Autry, CEO of a Fortune 500 company, recognized that by offering someone a chance to be part of the solution, he was also stepping into the person's shoes. So besides problem-solving, he was also strengthening his relationship through empathy. Try this approach with your children, ministry team, coworkers, friends; see how it works for you.

- Failing to understand the other person's point of view is often the root of conflicts. Ideally, conflicts are best talked through person-to-person. Sometimes this is not feasible. At other times we might best work through the conflict internally before we approach the other person. A long tradition exists of writing a dialogue with someone as a help to resolve conflict. Writing a dialogue invites us to step into someone else's shoes and view a situation from his or her perspective. Also, the technique can be used as a form of interior role-playing, in which we carry on a dialogue with someone with whom we are in conflict, in love, etc. Try this:

  - List several people with whom you feel your relationship invites further exploration. These may be relationships from the past, present, or the hopeful future.

  - Sit quietly, relax. Center. Write the name of one person, and then just reflect on the person: what they look like, generally how you feel with him or her, and other feelings.

  - Next, after a period of quiet, enter into a dialogue with the person. Let it flow where it will. Greet the person, and then write the dialogue. You might want to start with a question; write their answer; then respond, and so on.

    Me: I am confused about our last conversation. Could you explain what happened?

    Other: Well, you asked about...

  - When you have finished the dialogue, note any feelings you had during the dialogue.

- ○ Read the script back to yourself—preferably aloud.
- ○ Write a brief description of the dialogue and your reactions.

- Moving out of our comfort zone may help us understand people or situations in important ways. Pope Francis rode public transportation in Buenos Aires; he stopped on the streets and visited with poor people. He wanted to put himself in their shoes in order to understand them. The TV show *Undercover Boss* attempts to do this. A CEO or company president goes undercover in her or his own company. They work in the factory as a trainee or make sales calls hoping to understand what their workers are experiencing in the company. By walking in their employees' shoes these executives discover many startling and often difficult-to-swallow lessons—all of which are valuable to the company.

My Public Radio station highlighted a program in the Twin Cities in which a group of pastors were trying to live on food stamps for one week. And many of us are acquainted with programs in which able-bodied children use a wheelchair or crutches for a period of time just to learn what others experience who must use them.

So, construct your own exercise in empathy. Volunteer at a food bank or shelter. Try eating with the amount of food assistance you would receive if you had to rely on it. Take the bus to work for a week instead of driving. If you are an executive or manager, work with a line worker or maintenance person. Listen to these people. They all have lessons to teach us about life, our organization, and even about God.

Final Reflection

"You can never understand someone unless you understand their point-of-view, climb in that person's skin or stand and walk in that person's shoes," Atticus Finch told Scout. Francis would certainly agree, although he might add, "When you climb into that person's skin, you meet Christ in new ways too." Or, as G. K. Chesterton said of Francis, by stepping into the shoes of others "he only saw the image of God multiplied but never monotonous."

Empathy requires discipline and generosity of soul. It is also essential in building strong relationships based on truth and mutual respect. These strong relationships are the building blocks of strong congregations, healthy families, vibrant communities, and the People of God.

3

Opening Mind and Heart

*T*his archetypal story about the beginning of Jesus' ministry exemplifies the importance of awareness in the life of a
servant leader.

> Jesus, full of the Holy Spirit, returned from the Jordan and
> was led by the Spirit in the wilderness, where for forty days
> he was tempted by the devil. He ate nothing at all during
> those days, and when they were over, he was famished. The
> devil said to him, "If you are the Son of God, command
> this stone to become a loaf of bread." Jesus answered him,
> "It is written, 'One does not live by bread alone.'"
> Then the devil led him up and showed him in an instant
> all the kingdoms of the world. And the devil said to him,
> "To you I will give their glory and all this authority. . . If
> you, then, will worship me, it will be yours." Jesus answered,
> "It is written, 'Worship the Lord your God, and serve only
> him'"...Then Jesus, filled with the power of the Spirit,
> returned to Galilee. (Luke 4:1-14)

Even Jesus needed time alone to ground himself in his calling, his values, his core beliefs, and his commitment to the
Good News. Without this grounding, leaders easily fall into
the classic temptations of greed for possessions and for power
over others. Time in the "wilderness" allows us to answer
that key spiritual question: Where am I?

Recall the story of Eve, Adam, the serpent, and the for-
bidden tree. After Adam and Eve eat the fruit of the tree,

they hear God walking in the garden and go off and try to hide. They know that they have done something wrong. As they crouch in the bushes, God calls out to them, "Where are you?" Now that may seem like a strange question coming from God, a God who clearly knew where they were.

The Jewish philosopher Martin Buber offers a wonderful insight into the story:

> Adam hides himself to avoid rendering accounts, to escape responsibility for his way of living. Every man [or woman] hides for this purpose, for every man is Adam [every woman Eve] and finds himself in Adam's situation.... This situation can be precisely defined as follows: Man cannot escape the eye of God, but in trying to hide from him, he is hiding from himself. True, in him too there is something that seeks him, but he makes it harder and harder for that "something" to find him. This question is designed to awaken man and destroy his system of hideouts; it is to show man to what pass he has come and to awaken in him the great will to get out of it. (Quoted in Koch, *Journalkeeping*)

Before we can live more freely and more wisely as servant leaders, we need to honestly answer God's question to Adam and Eve: "Where are you?" God knows, but often *we* don't.

In imitation of Jesus, Francis of Assisi embraced the challenge of seeking awareness in the wilderness. His first biographer, Thomas of Celano, tells us:

> Truly, in regard to all those things which the glorious father Francis intended to do and did, his safest refuge was frequent prayer. Although he worked with the most ardent zeal for the good of those around him, he nonetheless most diligently took pains lest he neglect to tend to himself in every pursuit of perfection. To this end, he sought out solitary places and made his abode in the wilderness;

but, while living among people, he went alone at night to deserted houses or churches....

Boldly, he chose such places, I say, so that he might keep guard over himself in prayer; there, he first learned what he later taught others. However, he learned not so that he might painstakingly invent words to speak, but that thus, above and beyond the ways of human learning, he might drink most fully of the richness of heavenly wisdom, in order that he might be full, not so much with words as with the power of the Spirit. (*FA:TS* 408)

Without this awareness and "power of the Spirit," leaders are too readily pushed along by automatic impulses, ill-considered information, and outright prejudice. If we wish to grow as servant leaders, we need to steadily ask this hard question, or versions of it: Where am I? Am I conscious of all that I really am, or do I live on automatic pilot? Have I worn my masks so long that I have forgotten my true self? Is this person I project who I really am? Do my decisions as a leader reflect my core values and beliefs?

Francis urged the friars to pray each day, but he also urged them to take extended periods for reflection, even composing "A Rule for Hermitages." He tells his brothers:

Let those who wish to stay in hermitages in a religious way be three brothers or, at the most, four; let two of these be "the mother" and have two "sons" or at least one. Let the two who are "mothers" keep the life of Martha and the two "sons" the life of Mary and let one have one enclosure in which each one may have his cell in which he may pray and sleep. (*FA:TS* 61)

Francis wanted his brothers to maintain the same balance of contemplation and action that he strove to maintain for himself. Like the great servant leaders before and after him,

Francis realized that action without reflection can be disparate, futile, or even destructive.

Robert Greenleaf and other contemporary servant leaders echo Francis' wisdom about awareness balanced with action. Jeffrey McCollum, director of organization development for Warner Lambert Consumer Healthcare, remarked, "Leadership balances what's inside of us (our desire for meaning and purpose, our values and our aspirations) with what shows up on the outside—our actions. When our actions are balanced and in alignment with our thoughts and values, we are acting authentically." McCollum then puts in business language what Francis would frame in a religious way. McCollum says that balance begins when:

1. I pay attention to my own spiritual life.

2. I reconcile my inner life with my outer life and seek to recover enchantment.

3. I am clear that what's important to me and use that as a basis for action.

4. I pay attention to my "soul" side as well as my "strategic" side by deepening my spiritual, emotional, and intellectual capacities. ("The Inside-Out Proposition," 329)

Franciscan servant leaders pay attention to their spiritual lives so that their actions flow from the graces and direction of the Holy Spirit, not ego, not whims, not greed, not ignorance.

Awareness takes discipline and intentionality, and with these we can grow in our awareness. Fortunately, we have teachers like Francis and others to guide us.

Learning Franciscan Awareness

• Keeping a journal has a long and proven history as a tool of awareness or personal reflection. On campaign against the German tribes, the Roman Emperor Marcus Aurelius (121-180 c. e.) would repair to his tent each night. There he would sit at his camp table and write his meditations on the day, his thoughts addressed to himself. Marcus Aurelius did not write his *Meditations* for publication, but rather to think through how he was conducting not his battles, but his life. He reflects, "Remember to retire into this little territory of your own, and above all do not distract or strain yourself. Be free, and look at things as a human, as a citizen, as a mortal.... Look within. Within is the fountain of good, and it will always bubble up, if you will ever dig." The *Meditations* of Marcus Aurelius are still being read among the great books of wisdom of western civilization. For Francis, when we look "within," we encounter Holy Wisdom.

- ° If you periodically just relax, breathe deeply, and recollect your recent life, then begin writing about the question "Where am I?" with an open heart, you stay more in tune with who you are. If you allow your heart to speak and let your feelings surface, you will know the shape of your spirituality. Then you can make the choices that need to be made to move toward a richer, more harmonious life. If you are blocked at some point, write the question "Where am I?" and then start writing again. You can pose particular areas of life for consideration:

  Where am I in my relationship with God?

  Where am I in my relationships with family? Friends? Enemies?

  Then continue with the question about nature, work, your body, and so on.

- ° Many people find writing a daily journal enhances their awareness. They keep in mind the wisdom of Polly Berrien Berendes, who said, "Everything that happens to you is your teacher. The secret is to learn to sit at the feet of your own life and be taught by it." We try to describe daily events—inside and outside, work, projects, feelings, problems, and awareness. We seek to record the experience as close to the actual occurrence as possible to hold it in memory for further reflection. This log is best done at the end of the day.

- ○ Another awareness practice is to write down three blessings at the end of every day. For servant leaders, this focuses our attention and energy on how we have served—how we have helped others grow freer, wiser, healthier, and more likely themselves to become servants. Allow yourself to be surprised. Surprise is the beginning of gratefulness, a kind of rousing that we may need to get accustomed to as a gradual way into gratitude. Benedictine Brother David Steindl-Rast says it wisely: "What counts on your path to fulfillment is that we remember the great truth that moments of surprise want to teach us: everything is gratuitous, everything is gift. The degree to which we are awake to this truth is the measure of our gratefulness. And gratefulness is the measure of our aliveness." (*Gratefulness, the Heart of Prayer*)

- ○ Finally, each of these journal-writing approaches may be addressed explicitly to God. Our "Most High and glorious God" is always present to us, so why not include God in our reflections. One description of prayer that I have found helpful is that "prayer is our awareness of God and response to that awareness." In the case of journaling, our writing can be a sort of spontaneous letter to God in which we acknowledge our awareness with "Dear God" and then open our heart and mind to our "Most High and glorious God" in our writing.

- Another useful practice is to simply sit in the presence of the Holy Spirit and ponder a question for which we need insight. We often do this quite unconsciously. Our minds quietly just start mulling over some issue without our intending to. This kind of awareness has been called unstructured meditation. Here are some simple steps:

  o Select a question or issue or relationship about which you wish some insight and for which you have energy. For instance, it might be a decision you need to make or a question about how to deal with a relationship. Many of our experiences and the issues that emerge from our day-to-day life can be the subject of these unstructured meditation times.

  o As much as possible make sure you will have some time for this reflection. Sit quietly. Recall the presence of the Holy Spirit within you.

  o Then pose the question or state the issue as clearly as you can. The question becomes the focus of the time. Ask the question or pose the issue, perhaps directly to the Holy Spirit. Then listen to your heart and mind respond. You are not so much expecting answers, but trying to reach some understanding of what is going on in you, how you feel, how you are responding, and what the issue is calling forth from your true self.

  o If you become distracted away from your question, gently ask it again and reconnect to it. Distractions are inevitable, so be patient.

  o You are seeking the guidance and wisdom of the Holy Spirit, not necessarily ready answers or blueprints for action. Some issues may be the subject of weeks of meditation. Recording the fruit of your meditation in your journal may prove useful.

  o Close your meditation with words of thanks.

- Franciscan Murray Bodo reminds us, "Where my gaze is, is where my heart is. Prayer is setting aside time to redirect my gaze toward the one who alone is worthy of all my attention and love. Like St. Francis, then, in reorienting my gaze, I paradoxically see everything else in a new light" (*Tales of St. Francis*). One ancient way of redirecting my gaze is meditation on a single word, which can be very effective in drawing us close to the "Most High and glorious God." This meditation form is common to most of the world's great religions. Its Christian formulation can be found in a book called *The Cloud of Unknowing* by an anonymous English priest of the fourteenth century. He explains centering prayer this way:

> If you want to gather all your desire into one simple word that the mind can easily retain, choose a short word rather than a long one. A one-syllable word such as "God" or "love" is best. But choose one that is meaningful to you. Then fix it in your mind so that it will remain there come what may. This word will be your defense in conflict and in peace. Use it to beat upon the cloud of darkness about you and to subdue all distractions. (Ed. by William Johnston)

Repeating the single word can be powerful. When fire breaks out, everyone is galvanized into action by one word, "Fire!" This one word penetrates all barriers to attention. Follow these steps to experience centering meditation.

- ○ First, sit relaxed and still yourself by stretching and breathing deeply.

- ○ Then choose a single, sacred word that somehow expresses your deepest values. It might be a name of God [e.g., Holy Spirit, Wisdom, Jesus, Love, Light] or another sacred word: peace, hope.

- ○ Begin repeating this word or short phrase inwardly in harmony with your breathing.

○ If your mind wanders or you get distracted, gently start repeating your holy word(s) again.

○ End with some expression of gratitude and/or a smile.

Final Reflection

Parker Palmer, teacher and writer of such books as *The Active Life* and *The Courage to Teach*, commented about the sort of leadership we need today: "New leadership is needed for new times, but it will not come from finding new and more wily ways to manipulate the external world. It will come as we who lead find the courage to take an inner journey toward both our shadows and our light, a journey that, faithfully pursued, will take us beyond ourselves to become healers of a wounded world." This "new leadership" is grounded in awareness, the same kind of awareness great spiritual teachers like Francis, Clare, Benedict, and Jesus cultivated in themselves and encouraged in their followers.

4

Healing the Body of Christ

*W*e slice our finger while chopping tomatoes. We grow angry at another person and say things for which we're later sorry. The relationship dies as a result. If we have lived long enough, we have grieved over the loss of someone we loved.

Suffering comes in many forms. Depression. Grief. Physical illness. Broken relationships. We live, we suffer. And healing may come in just as many forms. The kindness of friends. Acts of reconciliation. Capable medical care. Forgiveness.

To hope for and seek healing are inherent human traits. Our cut finger automatically tends to bind itself. The blood begins to clot and glands in our skin release an antiseptic fluid to kill germs. Our blood and skin immediately start the healing process. In relationships, grief or guilt moves us to bind broken connections. In short, we seek healing. Servant leaders, too, by definition, seek to heal. As Greenleaf said, they want those served to "grow as persons" and "become healthier."

Suffering means dis-ease, dis-integration, dis-function, incoherence, contradiction, defeat. The word "health" comes from an old Saxon word that means "hale" or "whole." All the many separate parts of the person, community, or organization work in harmony, functioning smoothly together. "Healing" then indicates effort to make whole or to enhance the harmonious, balanced functioning of the entire human being, community, or organization.

People who are new to servant leadership may tend to shy away from thinking of themselves as healers, but healing is integral both to living the Good News and walking in the footsteps of Francis and other servant leaders. The challenge for many of us is to move past the narrow images we have of healing. Yes, it is a miracle, but it is more ubiquitous than we think. Most servant leaders tend to be healers without even knowing it. They seek to patch up hurting relationships. They do not fear forgiveness. They step in when someone needs a hand or a caring listener. All these actions can bring healing: *making whole again.*

Jesus named healing as central proof that he was "the one"—the savior of humankind. He told John the Baptist's disciples, "Go and tell John what you hear and see: the blind receive their sight, the lame walk, the lepers are cleansed, the deaf hear, the dead are raised, and the poor have good news brought to them" (Matt. 11:4-5). In Luke's gospel, Jesus declares to his followers: God "has anointed me to bring good news to the poor. He has sent me to proclaim release to the captives and recovery of sight to the blind, to let the oppressed go free" (4:18). Healing is what servant leaders did when Jesus lived, when Francis lived, and now in our lifetimes.

Like Jesus, Francis preached and healed. The stories of his healings fill biographies written about him. In a long list of healing stories, Bonaventure includes these two:

> There was a woman in the town of Gubbio whose both hands were so withered and crippled that she could do nothing with them. When he made the sign of the cross over them in the name of the Lord, she was so perfectly cured that she immediately went home and prepared with her own hands food for him and for the poor, like Peter's mother-in-law.

In the village of Bevagna he marked the eyes of a blind girl with his saliva three times in the name of the Trinity and restored the sight she longed for. (*FA:TF* 627)

Note that the woman prepared a meal for Francis, but also "the poor." Healing is not just for the one healed. Servant leaders heal so that those healed can more likely become servants themselves.

Francis not only healed broken bodies, but sought to bring peace to broken relationships. Thomas of Celano reports that "In all of his preaching, before he presented the word of God to the assembly, he prayed for peace saying, 'May the Lord give you peace.'... Accordingly, many *who hated peace* along with salvation, with the Lord's help wholeheartedly embraced peace. They became themselves children of peace" (*FA:TS*, 203). In "A Prayer Inspired by the Our Father," Francis urges the brothers to offer peace even to enemies:

> As we forgive those who trespass against us:
> And what we do not completely forgive,
> make us, Lord, forgive completely
> that we may truly love our enemies because of You
> and we may fervently intercede for them
> before You,
> returning no one evil for evil
> and we may strive to help everyone in You.
> (*FA:TS* 159)

Francis also strove to make peace in broken communities. In Bologna, he moved the arguing factions to make a new peace treaty. In Arezzo and Sienna, Francis helped end bloodshed between warring parties. Leonardo Boff recounts Francis' peacemaking efforts in Assisi itself:

> The bishop had excommunicated the mayor, and he, in turn, had prohibited the buying and selling of anything to the

bishop. Francis saw what was happening and, troubled, said: "It is a great shame for us, servants of the Lord, that the bishop and the mayor hate each other in this way, without anyone bothering to pacify them." (*Saint Francis*)

Even though he was near death, Francis sent the brothers to bring the mayor and bishop together. When they met, the friars began singing a stanza from the "Canticle of the Creatures," in which Francis refers to the dispute. Hearing the verse, the mayor and the bishop were reconciled and embraced each other as friends.

If servant leaders have listened, walked in others' shoes, and grown in awareness, they may effectively help heal broken hearts, bodies, and relationships. This, of course, is not only the right thing to do, but is an important thing to do if the community or organization is to thrive and produce good.

Healing leaders often go unnoticed, and that is fine with these women and men. But every once in a great while we have a very public example of healing by a corporate executive. One outsized example was owner and CEO of Malden Mills, Aaron Feuerstein. The company, makers of Polartec, burned to the ground. The fire destroyed not only the building but, more important, 3,000 jobs and one of the few remaining manufacturing companies in Lawrence, Massachusetts. Instead of taking the insurance money and retiring, Feuerstein rebuilt and paid employees until they reopened. Many corporations thought him foolish. Feuerstein, with the heart of a healer coupled with the mind of a smart executive said, "I have a responsibility to the worker, both blue-collar and white-collar. I have an equal responsibility to the community. It would have been unconscionable to put 3,000 people on the streets and deliver a death blow to the cities of Lawrence and Methuen." Eventually, in his late seventies, Feuerstein relinquished control of the company, and while the old Malden Mills dissolved, employees began a new company that still makes Polartec products.

Aaron Feuerstein's story has been used widely as an example of servant leaders striving to heal broken hearts and fractured communities. He wanted to help make things whole again. Many forces seek to divide us and polarize, but servant leaders heal. This is one reason that Abraham Lincoln's "House Divided" speech remains one of the most important and prescient speeches in U.S. history. A country divided between slave states and free states could not remain whole. The Civil War demonstrated the tragedy of a house divided. Of course, Lincoln was quoting Mark 3:25: "If a house is divided against itself, that house will not be able to stand." This timeless truth applies to any company, community, or organization that is rife with conflict, disorganization, loss of focus and values, and toxic competition. A person divided within himself or herself cannot stand either.

Contemporary leaders are embracing what Lincoln, Jesus, and Francis knew about healing and servant leadership. Having been president of two state universities, Judith Sturnick now heads The Sturnick Group for Executive Coaching and Consulting to Corporations, Higher Education and Healthcare. She sums up the role of healing in servant leadership this way: "Healing Leadership," she says "has meaning on at least two levels: restoring our leaders by bringing them back to emotional, spiritual, intellectual, and physical health; and from the wisdom and insight gained through that healing process to provide, in turn, leadership that heals and transforms the quality of life and work within our organizations."

Servant leaders and servant followers both need healing or wholeness to thrive and be about God's business. The servant leader is called to set an example of healing.

Learning Franciscan Healing

- HALT is a handy acronym that comes from twelve-step programs. The letters stand for Hungry, Angry, Lonely, Tired. Use HALT as a way of monitoring and remembering good self-care principles. If you feel rundown, HALT. Take a minute to ask yourself four questions. Am I hungry? Am I angry? Am I lonely? Am I tired? If you can say "yes" to any one of these, do something about it before continuing your day. If you can say "yes" to more than one of these, you've probably gone too far already, and tending to your healing is more important than ever.

- We have all likely heard about forty-something executives who have died of heart attacks, slumped over their desks. Or perhaps we've watched once-slim friends hit fifty having doubled their weight. At the end of his life, Francis apologized to his body for having so mistreated it. He healed others, but took too little care of his own health. Servant leaders should not be obsessed about their health, but it is easy to pay it too little attention. Some statements that are commonly used to describe good health habits are listed below. Ask yourself how you are doing in each area. If you are doing okay, be thankful. If you want to make some modifications, jot down some action steps that you can take; be sure that they are realistic:

  ○ I eat healthy foods, especially vegetables, fruit, whole-grain, high-fiber breads and cereals, lean meat, and low-fat dairy products.

  ○ I limit my consumption of fats and cholesterol-rich foods.

  ○ I exercise for twenty to thirty minutes at least three times each week.

  ○ I maintain a healthy weight.

- º I enjoy sufficient quality time with friends and family.
- º I don't smoke and I stay away from smoky environments.
- º I'm a moderate drinker of alcoholic beverages if I drink at all.
- º I have developed leisure activities that I find relaxing and energizing.
- º I keep track of medications that I take and do what I can to need less and less of them.
- º I try to bring joy and meaning to my work.
- º I express my feelings clearly, but appropriately, rather than swallowing them.
- º I have learned stress-reducing strategies.
- º I wear a seat belt and drive safely.
- º I read and try to keep learning.
- º I pray and reflect regularly.
- º I receive an annual physical (especially significant for those over age forty), and maintain awareness of any conditions that run in my family.

- Lingering, toxic anger can tear us apart. Holding on to anger with all its bitterness and not forgiving has been described as drinking poison myself and hoping that it will kill my enemy. The Reverend Harry Emerson Fosdick declared that "hating and not forgiving people is like burning down your own house to get rid of a rat." Just as Francis sought to make peace among warring factions, our health urges us to make peace within ourselves.

  In short, servant leader healers need to learn forgiveness, which Robert Enright at the Wisconsin Center on Forgiveness described as "giving up the resentment to which you are entitled, and offering to the persons who hurt you friendlier attitudes to which they are not entitled." We can forgive and begin to heal by our own actions. Reconciliation takes both parties and so may never happen, but healing comes with forgiveness that requires only my will and God's help.

- ○ Spend a few minutes recalling an event in which you were hurt or betrayed or deeply disappointed. Then, in your own words, write to the Holy One about your anger, resentment, rage, or hurt. Express all your feelings of anger and desire for revenge. Then end your writing by inviting the Most High and Glorious God to be the judge and jury. Surrender your right to retribution to the Creator of the universe. (You may not want to forget what happened and what you learned, but you can still forgive. Be patient, though. Healing of deep hurts may take a long time and more prayer.)

- Richard Nielsen, professor of management at Boston College, teaches what he calls "Friendly Disentangling" as a method of conflict resolution. This method has deep roots in the Quaker tradition of peacemaking. Francis would likely understand it immediately because of its central premise contained in this Quaker motto: "Walk cheerfully over the earth answering that of Go(o)d in everyone." As a Quaker, Robert Greenleaf both used and taught this four-step method:

1. Begin by centering on the Go(o)d in all the participants in the conflict while trying to frame the conflict in terms of the "biases of an embedded tradition" that "we" are all part of; think of the situation as *our* challenge. For instance, leaders sometimes must deal with workplace rules that have a long history, but are viewed as no longer helpful. To disentangle the situation, a healer seeks to focus attention on the history and the rules to

understand them, keeping clearly in mind that all the people involved are part of the solution and inherently Go(o)d.

2. All participants should be dealt with in a friendly manner. Greenleaf invited people to tell their stories and share their common experiences working well together. When the founder of Southwest Airlines, Herb Kelleher, entered discussions with the unions about a new contract, he was present at all the sessions and, even after tough talks, took both sides out to dinner. Kelleher knew that the company depended on all employees working well together — not "divided against themselves."

3. Invite all participants to help disentangle the problematic behavior from the traditional way of doing things. All too often, we operate automatically on assumptions and procedures that may have once worked just fine, but may not work as well now. Everyone should be asked to disentangle the systems at work.

4. Finally, ask willing participants to experiment with alternatives to the activities or beliefs that have not been effective. In other words, invite people to explore new ways of doing things and let those willing try these new ways. Everyone can be asked to be part of the evaluation before more lasting changes go into effect. For example, while at AT&T, Greenleaf noticed that there were few African-American managers. After implementing steps 1, 2, and 3, the team came up with several approaches to hiring, developing, or promoting African-American managers. No quotas or hard and fast goals were set, but over time with the consciousness raised on the issue and trying some different approaches, the number of African-American managers went up tenfold.

Think of some conflict in your organization, family, business, or community that needs healing. Try this "friendly disentanglement" method.

• Looking at our organizational policies and benefits may help us head off conflicts and situations that would call for healing later on. Here are a few things to consider:

  ○ Healthcare plans: Does our healthcare plan include preventative benefits? Are part-time workers included? Servant leader companies try to offer part-time workers a health plan because they depend on these workers and healthy workers are more productive and loyal.

  ○ Policy manuals: Most policies and procedures are formulated to deal with a tiny percentage of people who will probably ignore them in any case. Servant leaders approach matters by asking The Golden Rule question: If I were in this situation, how would I want to be treated? Healing leaders may want to look at policies and procedures to be sure that they include only absolutely essential policies and only ones that treat colleagues as respected adults.

  ○ Quiet Acts of Kindness: Leaders can also promote healing by many small acts of kindness. For instance, when he was CEO of Meredith Corporation, Jim Autry would come in early to write birthday, sympathy, or thank-you cards to employees. Employees at Southwest Airlines can expect sympathy notes from the leadership when a pet dies. They also know that leaders in the company will try to ensure that they have the time they need to get well or take care of a very sick child or parent. The founder and CEO of SAS Institute, James Goodnight, remarked: "Ninety-five percent of our assets drive out the gate every afternoon at five. I want them to come back in the morning. I need them to come back in the morning." A healing servant leader recognizes that the health of any organization depends on the health of the people, so he or she looks for even small ways to keep people healthy.

Final Reflection

Robert Greenleaf often reminded people that the word *religion* means "to rebind" or to make whole. Servant leadership, like religion, seeks "to bridge the separation between persons and the cosmos, to heal the widespread alienation, and to reestablish men and women in the role of servants—*healers*—of society." Included in Greenleaf's perspective is also the need for individuals to be whole, too—through balanced lives of awareness and action.

Jesus and his follower Francis provide a model of healing for servant leaders. To act as they did would be to act as God does. Their typical injunction to the disciples is to heal. Jesus commands his disciples to go out to the whole world: "As you go, proclaim the good news, 'The reign of heaven has come near.' Cure the sick, raise the dead, cleanse the lepers, cast out demons" (Matthew 10:7-8). For the modern servant leader the invitation is the same.

5

Drawing All to God's Reign

"*P*reach the Gospel at all times—if necessary, use words" is a saying that is commonly attributed to Francis. Although this particular statement is not found anywhere in the verified writings or remarks of Francis, it makes an important point: Example preaches the Gospel more powerfully than words alone. Of course, Francis also preached eloquently with words, songs, and conversation. During his lifetime, the friars spread out across the known world to preach and teach the Gospels. They wanted to change minds and hearts, to bring people to life in Christ: that is, they sought to persuade. They could only be persuasive, however, if the lives they led matched the words they spoke.

Leaders influence people to do things. Influence can occur through coercion, manipulation, positional authority, or persuasion. The type of leadership being exercised is evidenced by the ways in which decisions are made and how those who lead compel others to take action. Dictators typically use their positional authority and manipulation or coercion to see that things get done. Servant leaders like Jesus, Francis, and executives at servant leader companies like Vanguard, SAS Institute, and Southwest Airlines look to persuasion as the first and best means of moving followers to get things done.

Persuasion empowers followers because it acknowledges that they have talents, ideas, and skills absolutely essential to

71

the success of the organization. Persuasion is the exercise of power *with* others. Coercion and manipulation exert power *over* other people, in effect telling them that their ideas and points of view are useless, second-rate, and ignorable: "If I want your opinion, I'll give it to you." Manipulation may seem more benign than outright coercion, but its intent is still the same—to move people to do things that the manipulator wants them to do even if the action is bad for them. Both power *with* others and power *over* others are types of power, but only the first is the power of servant leadership, the power of Francis and Jesus.

The word *power* comes from the Latin *posse* or French *poeir*, meaning "to be able." Power can be our ability to coerce, brow beat, manipulate, and kill. Power is also our ability to breathe, cry for help, feed ourselves, work the fields, write articles, and love. What distinguishes servant leader power is that it is power *with* others. Greenleaf explains, "In a complex institution-centered society...there will be large and small concentrations of power. Sometimes it will be a servant's power of persuasion and example. Sometimes it will be coercive power used to dominate and manipulate people. The difference is that, in the former, power is used to create opportunity and alternatives that individuals may choose and build autonomy. In the latter, individuals are coerced." For Greenleaf, the only legitimate power is power *with*.

Jesus and Francis utilized their own gifts and insights in their exertion of power to persuade and inspire others. In his directions to the "ministers" of his order—Francis did not call them "superiors"—he says that the friars who have a hard time observing the Rule should seek out the ministers. He tells the ministers to "receive them charitably and kindly and have such familiarity with them that these same brothers may speak and deal with them as masters with their servants, for so it must be that the ministers are the servants of all the brothers" (*FA:TS* 105). Taking this approach, the ministers helped the friars work through their difficulties rather than robbing them of their responsibility and ability to grow in Gospel living.

One story that speaks to Francis as a persuasive servant leader concerns his dealing with the bishop of Imola:

> He went to the bishop of the city and humbly asked, according to his pleasure, to be able to call the people together to preach to them. The bishop replied harshly to him: "Brother, I preach to my people and that is enough!" The genuine humble man bowed his head and went outside, but less than an hour later he came back in. At this, since the bishop was annoyed, he asked him what he was looking for a second time. He responded with a humility of heart as well as of voice: "My lord, if a father throws his son out by one door, he should come back by another." The bishop, overcome by humility, embraced him with a smile, saying: "From now on, you and all your brothers have my general permission to preach in my diocese, because your holy humility has earned it." (*FA:TF* 574)

Francis understood the bishop and clearly respected him. By coming back and alluding to Matthew 7:9—"Is there anyone among you who, if your child asks for bread, will give a stone?"—Francis acknowledges the dignity of the bishop and his right to grant a gift. He also persuades by reminding the bishop that Jesus would grant the requests of his followers when they asked.

Francis employed the model of persuasion that Christ used with the disciples on the road to Emmaus. Recall the story from Luke 24:13-35. Two of the disciples were walking the seven miles to Emmaus, talking about the betrayal of Jesus, his death on the cross, and the mysterious happenings at his tomb. Jesus joined them on the road, but they didn't recognize him. The story continues: "'What are you discussing with each other while you walk along?' They stood still, looking sad.... 'Are you the only stranger in Jerusalem who does not know the things that have taken place here in these days?' He asked them, 'What things?'" The two disciples recount Jesus' story from their point of view: They thought he was the One, but he was crucified. Their hopes were dashed. Now "some women" said Christ had risen and was alive.

Having listened to their understanding of events, Jesus broadens their awareness."Beginning with Moses and all the prophets, he interpreted to them the things about himself in all the scriptures." Despite this explanation, the two disciples still do not quite get it. Even so, they invite Jesus to stay with them and have some food: "When he was at table with them, he took bread, blessed and broke it, and gave it to them. Then their eyes were opened, and they recognized him.... They said to each other, 'Were not our hearts burning within us?'"

Jesus changed their minds and enflamed their hearts. He persuaded first by understanding them, then offering them truth from scripture that they could understand. They finally comprehended who he was when they invited him into fellowship with them in the breaking of the bread. This is servant leadership persuasion: listening empathetically, respecting people where they are, raising awareness and understanding, healing, and opening people to positive change.

Highly successful corporations and organizations have learned servant leadership persuasion and have shown how it is not only the right way to lead but is the most effective way too. As senior vice-president of the Sisters of St. Joseph Health System in Ann Arbor, Michigan, Sister Joyce De-Shano explained: "Servant leadership is the power to influence rather than the power to control. We realize that when we choose to influence people rather than control them, it at first might seem like weakness, but it really calls forth an inner strength. We think it really serves to engage and develop the creativity, productivity, and vibrancy that already exist in the regions." She concludes that this leadership style will improve her organization's ability to meet the critical challenges of health care provision and administration (quoted in Spears, *Insights on Leadership*).

Persuasion in the service of good empowers, creates buy-in, can enliven spirits, and is in the long run more effective, so that all members of the community might be able to feel their hearts "burning within them."

Learning Franciscan Persuasion

* Ponder—perhaps in writing—each of these principles that undergird the approach to persuasion of a servant leader:

    1. For people to feel empowered to use all their skills and experience for a common good, communities or organizations provide an environment that allows them to be creative, to experiment, and to trust.

    2. Servant leaders recognize that personal growth and organizational development are intertwined.

    3. Servant leaders know that individuals make a difference and ensure that all individuals know this fact too.

    Use these questions to guide your reflection:

    ○ Do I really believe in these approaches?

    ○ Would any of my actions show others in my organization that these are principles that I actually hold?

* Effective teachers know that explaining to students the benefits of doing their math homework is much more effective than just ordering them to do it. Factory supervisors know that helping coworkers understand the rationale behind a change in procedure ensures better implementation than simply ordering them to do things differently; better, if workers had input into the changes, effective implementa-

tion is even more likely. Here are some parts in the process of persuasion; they are not numbered because some parts may occur simultaneously:

○ *Formulate an idea for action* about which you need to persuade others; it does not have to be fully formulated. Indeed, you might want to persuade people to work with you to begin discussion of something of use to the community: for example, a group of advocates for single seniors unable to take care of their finances or setting up daycare for employees within your company's facility. Keep in mind Greenleaf's description of the goal of servant leaders: The servant leader makes "sure that other people's highest priority needs are being served. The best test, and difficult to administer, is: Do those served grow as persons? Do they, *while being served*, become healthier, wiser, freer, more autonomous, more likely themselves to become servants? *And*, what is the effect on the least privileged in society; will they benefit, or, at least, not be further deprived?"

○ *Establish Credibility*: Do some solid homework about the issue, so that you have a groundwork of knowledge, even if the action plan is in its infancy. Listen to a wide range of people's ideas about the topic. Face-to-face conversations add to your credibility as a leader on the issue, especially when people see you taking them seriously. Credibility develops from two sources: expertise and relationships. The more people are involved early in the discussion and formulation, the more likely it is that your eventual plan will not demand a lot of persuading.

○ *Understand Your Audience.* Who are the people involved in the issue? What would be the benefits to all parties? What challenges? Whose buy-in is absolutely essential? Again, knowing the participants requires conversations. Be prepared to make revisions to any preliminary notions you started with.

○ *Revise Your Plan.* By this point, you will have received valuable input from people, your research, and your own intuition. Revise accordingly.

○ *Prepare Your Supporting Evidence and Polish the Communications.* What stories, images, graphs of data, and examples can you use to make your case? Recall that Jesus used parables or stories when preaching, as did Francis. Your point will become vivid with strong examples and solid evidence.

○ *Use the Full Range of Communication Tools that are Effective with Your Audience.* Memos from a working group with a well-formulated rationale, posted on a bulletin board, may persuade some people that your idea has benefits for the common good. Today, though, an online video or catchy use of social media may be more effective with more people. The wider variety of methods of communicating your plan or ideas, the more likely it is that they will be embraced.

Final Reflection

Jesus, Francis, and other servant leaders recognize that true change comes once people open their hearts to change. This is the power of the Holy Spirit. Bonaventure says of Francis:

Through divine prompting the man of God began to become a model of evangelical perfection and to invite others to penance. His statements were...filled with the power of the Holy Spirit, they penetrated the marrow of the heart, so that they moved those hearing them in stunned amazement. In all his preaching, he announced peace by saying: "May the Lord give you peace."...

Thus it happened that,
filled with the spirit of the prophets
and according to a prophetic passage,
he proclaimed peace,
preached salvation,
and, by counsels of salvation,
brought to true peace
many who had previously lived at odds with Christ
and far from salvation.

(FA:TF, 543)

As servant leaders, we too can bring peace and good to the world by developing our skills of persuasion, so that people may grow freer, healthier, wiser, and more likely to become servants of a common good.

6

Gospel Vision

"Not much happens without a dream," Robert Greenleaf remarked. "And for something great to happen, there must be a great dream. Behind every great achievement is a dreamer of great dreams. Much more than a dreamer is required to bring it to reality; but the dream must be there first." Francis was certainly one such great dreamer. His vision or concept of what he was called to be and do was simple, but profound and compelling.

The first part of his call came with his encounter with God in the decrepit San Damiano Chapel. From the crucifix, he heard God's invitation: "Francis, go and repair my house which, as you see, is all being destroyed" (*FA:TF* 536). He immediately answered this call and spent the rest of his life inviting others to help him rebuild the Church.

When more and more men joined Francis, he formulated the other expression of his mission. Bonaventure recounts, "Christ's servant wrote for himself and his brothers a form of life in simple words in which...he had placed the observance of the holy Gospel as its unshakable foundation" (*FA:TF* 547). In The Later Rule, his focus on the Gospels had not changed: The heart of the rule is "to observe the Holy Gospel of Our Lord Jesus Christ by living in obedience, without anything of one's own, and in chastity" (*FA:TS* 100).

Live the Gospels; rebuild the Church. This was the mission and rule that guided all of Francis' decisions and formed his charism. Many church authorities urged him, and even later tried to manipulate the friars, to adopt one of the older rules. Nevertheless, Francis embraced this calling in all its directness, simplicity, and power. In 1209 or 1210, Francis walked to Rome to request that Pope Innocent III approve his rule. The following scene unfolded:

> He explained his proposal, humbly and urgently imploring him to approve that rule of life.... [Innocent III] gave his assent to the pious request. Yet he hesitated to do what Christ's little poor man asked because it seemed to some of the cardinals to be something novel and difficult beyond human powers.
>
> ...Inspired by the Holy Spirit, John of St. Paul, Bishop of Sabina, said to the Supreme Pontiff and his brother cardinals: "If we refuse the request of this poor man as novel or too difficult, when all he asks is to be allowed to lead the Gospel life, we must be on our guard lest we commit an offense against Christ's Gospel. For if anyone says that there is something novel or irrational or impossible to observe in this man's desire to live according to the perfection of the Gospel, he would be guilty of blasphemy against Christ, the author of the Gospel." (*FA:TF* 547)

The Pope agreed. The rule was approved. Francis and his band of friars would strive to live the Gospels, and as a result, rebuild the Church.

At the heart of living the Gospels is building the Reign of God. Jesus told his followers, "Do not worry about your life, what you will eat or what you will drink, or about your body, what you will wear.... Strive first for the kingdom of God and his righteousness and all these things will be given to you as well" (Matthew 6:26-34). What we "set our heart on"—our creed—gives shape to our actions, and our actions shape our lives. An old adage says:

Plant an act; reap a habit.
Plant a habit; reap a virtue or vice.
Plant a virtue or vice; reap a character.
Plant a character; reap a destiny.

What we believe—where we direct our heart—sets the course of our destiny. Francis and followers of Christ set their hearts on the Reign of God and God's justice.

What does this Reign of God look like? The prophet Isaiah announces that the Christ will have "the spirit of wisdom and understanding.... Righteousness shall be the belt around his waist, and faithfulness the belt around his loins." Then Isaiah provides a vivid description of the Reign of God:

The wolf shall live with the lamb, the leopard shall lie down with the kid,
the calf and the lion and the fatling together,
and a little child shall lead them....
The nursing child shall play over the hole of the asp, and the weaned child shall put its hand on the adder's den.
They will not hurt or destroy on all my holy mountain;
for the earth will be full of the knowledge of the Lord.
(11:1-9)

For Francis, following Jesus' footsteps, the Reign of God can only come when people follow the central Law of the Gospels.

Francis' vision of living the Gospels is summarized by the two great commandments. In his Later Admonitions, he tells the friars:

How happy and blessed are those who love God and do as the Lord Himself says in the Gospel: You shall love the Lord your God with all your heart and all your mind, and your neighbor as yourself. (*FA:TS*, 46)

Live the Gospel; Rebuild the Church was Francis' vision for himself and the friars, and this would only be accomplished by love.

Great servant leaders like Francis may express their visions for the Good Life in different words, but they all conceptualize a life in which people's "highest priority needs" are met, and they become "healthier, freer, wiser, and more autonomous, and more likely themselves to become servants." Greenleaf adds that the servant leader always asks, "What is the effect on the least privileged in society; will they benefit, or, at least, not be further deprived?" Francis poses the same question after urging the brothers to love their neighbors as themselves: "And if anyone does not want to love them as himself, let him at least not do them any harm, but let him do good" (*FA:TS* 47). Centuries apart in time, Greenleaf and Francis have kindred visions of what it means to serve, to love, to live the Gospels — to be servant leaders.

Visionaries like Francis are always in great demand and short supply. Those who seek to become Franciscan servant leaders are needed now. Warren Bennis, author of *On Becoming a Leader*, remarked: "In the twenty-first century, we will need leaders who know what is important in the long term. Who have a vision, dream, mission, or strategic intent. Who remind people continually of what's important and create an environment where people know why they are there." Francis calls us back to the Gospels, so we know what's important and why we are here.

Learning Franciscan Gospel Vision

- Our core beliefs tell us where "our heart is." To conceptualize our vision and mission, we can start by identifying these core beliefs. Write at least two core beliefs — central meanings and values — around each area of life. Of course this is a working document that you will likely revise.

- ○ God

  I believe...
  I believe...

- ○ Relationships with Other People

  I believe...
  I believe...

- ○ Body and Sexuality

  I believe...
  I believe...

- ○ Suffering and Death

  I believe...
  I believe...

- ○ Work and Vocation

  I believe...
  I believe...

- ○ Nature and the Environment

  I believe...
  I believe...

Now try to pull all these beliefs together into your Creed: a summary of your most closely held beliefs.

- Next, write a Personal Mission Statement. It helps us identify

  a) who we want to be

  b) what we want to do

  c) to what and to whom we want to devote our life

  d) the principles to which we want to anchor our life

  e) the legacy we want to leave

Here are some famous mission statements:

- Abraham Lincoln: "Preserve the Union"
- Nelson Mandela: "End Apartheid"
- Mother Theresa: "Show mercy and compassion to the dying"
- Joan of Arc: "Free France"
- Henry Ford: "Democratize the automobile"
- Jesus: "To bring good news to the poor, proclaim release to the captives and recovery of sight to the blind, to let the oppressed go free"

When composing your mission statement, challenge yourself to be as expansive as Francis! As Jesus!

- Two Exercises to Formulate a Mission Statement:

    1. Close your eyes. Try to visualize the following: You've lived a fulfilling, rewarding life, and it is now your eightieth birthday. Imagine that all of the people you love are there to celebrate with you and pay you tribute. There are people from your personal and professional life, and friends and neighbors from the community. What would you like them to say? In other words, what do you want to be remembered for? Start by writing the tribute you would like to receive from each person.

    2. Jon Kabat-Zinn, author of *Wherever You Go, There You Are*, suggests posing this question to ourselves in order to arrive at some sense of our mission: "What is my job on the planet?" There are really two elements to explore in the question. First, what is *my job*? We waste much of our lives doing someone else's job, trying to meet other people's

expectations, listening to a cacophony of voices all telling us who we should be and what we should do. My job is JOB with a capital J, the JOB that only I can do. The JOB each person has is more than the paid employment that he or she does; that may be part of the JOB, but probably only a part. Parenting their children is part of any parents' JOB. A heart surgeon's JOB might include her special way of careful listening that she offers each patient. By uncovering our particular talents, gifts, skills, and stories in writing, we begin to understand and appropriate many of the qualities that are part of our JOB. With these things in mind, free-write an answer to the question "What is my job on the planet?"

o Finally, in one or two sentences, write a personal mission statement taking into account your "tribute" and/or your "JOB in the universe" statement: Post this Personal Mission Statement so that you can read it every day, like Gandhi did: "Let the first act of every morning be to make the following resolve for the day: I shall not fear anyone on Earth. I shall fear only God. I shall not bear ill toward anyone. I shall not submit to injustice from anyone. I shall conquer untruth by truth. And in resisting untruth, I shall put up with all suffering."

• Matching Visions: Ponder the mission statement of your organization, school, company, or community. Consider each element. How do you feel about it? Does it seem energizing? Does it provide focus? Does it have a positive effect on you? Then review your personal mission statement in light of the corporate mission statement. Do the two have much in common? Do they contradict in any important ways? If you support the corporate mission are you compromising your personal mission statement? What are points of congruence?

Final Reflections

Proverbs 29:18 declares: "Where there is no vision the people get out of hand" (NJB). Vision plays a crucial role in keeping a community's eyes on the prize. Vision begins with our thoughts that lead to action; actions build our character and, ultimately, our future. The philosopher Heraclitus said: "The soul is dyed the color of its thoughts. Think only on those things that are in line with your principles and can bear the full light of day. The content of your character is your choice. Day by day what you choose, what you think, and what you do is who you become. Your integrity is your destiny—it is the light that guides your way."

Francis' light was the Gospels. He immersed himself in them and made them central to his long periods of prayer. They formed his vision, which drew women and men to follow him. In doing so, they rebuilt the church of his day and continue to rebuild the church and world of our day. He invites us to ask for this vision in his prayer based on the Lord's Prayer:

Your kingdom come:
That You may rule in us through Your grace
and enable us to come to Your kingdom
where there is clear vision of You,
perfect love of You...

.....

Your will be done on earth as in heaven:
That we may love You...
and by seeking Your glory in everything,...
we may love our neighbor as ourselves
by drawing them all to Your love with our whole
strength,
by rejoicing in the good of others as in our own,
by suffering with others at their misfortunes,
and by giving offense to no one.

(*FA:TS* 158-159)

7

Attending Now, Looking Ahead

*I*n 1220, Francis resigned as leader of the community of little brothers. They had assembled at the Porziuncola for their annual meeting, or chapter. His health was declining, and the community had grown large and spread far and wide. In addition, during the chapter, the pope instructed the community to appoint guardians for each local group, require a year-long novitiate before admission, and establish permanent vows. While honoring the pope's directives and realizing that changes in the community were inevitable, Francis also recognized that he was not the one to impose the new order. He also sadly foresaw increasing tensions among the friars about a movement among some of the friars away from the ideal of total poverty. Consequently, he relinquished his leadership role so that he could return to the simple life of a friar.

Thomas of Celano tells the story this way:

> He resigned the office of prelate before all the brothers of the religion, saying: "From now on, I am dead to you. But here you have Brother Peter of Catanio; let us all, you and I, obey him." And bowing down immediately, he promised him "obedience and reverence." The brothers were weeping, and sorrow drew deep groans from them, as they saw themselves orphaned of such a father.

As blessed Francis got up, he joined his hands and, lifting his eyes to heaven, said: "Lord, I give back to you the family which until now you have entrusted to me. Now, sweetest Lord, because of my infirmities, which you know, I can no longer take care of them and I entrust them to the ministers." (*FA:TF*, 340)

From this time forward, Francis "remained subject until his death" and a servant leader to the friars. He foresaw that his true effectiveness would not be as "prelate," but as guide, example, and servant.

Francis demonstrated a trait of servant leaders by astutely observing the life around him. He further held his observations before the light of the Gospels during long periods of prayer. His concern about the friars seeking status as clerics or scholars had solid basis in what he saw happening. In addition, "he saw many rushing for positions of authority." Having relinquished his own position of authority, "he strove by example to call them back from such sickness" (*FA:TS* 273). Francis lived simply, but he was hardly naïve about what could tear the friars apart in the future.

Up until the end of his life, Francis exhorted the little brothers to hold fast to holy poverty and the rule that guided them. In his Testament, written near the time of his death, Francis held up his vision, lest there be any argument in the future about his true intentions:

Let the brothers be careful not to receive in any way churches or poor dwellings or anything else built for them unless they are according to the holy poverty we have promised in the Rule....

And let the general minister and all the other ministers and custodians be bound through obedience not to add to or take away from these words. And let them always have this writing with them together with the Rule.... And I strictly command all my cleric and lay brothers, through obedience, not to place any gloss upon the Rule. (*FA:TS* 126-127)

Francis knew he could not control the future, but based on his experience, he foresaw some of the challenges ahead for the brothers and did what he could to keep their hearts directed toward the Gospels.

Foresight may not be a quality popularly associated with Francis, but it could be argued that the community might not have survived if Francis had lacked that skill. Foresight is that ability to be totally "in the present" combined with a strong sense of how the present has been influenced by the past and that what happens now will have real consequences in the future. Greenleaf called foresight "the central ethic of leadership." Only by considering the consequences of a course of action can we ensure that our present decision will be the right one. Howard Johnson, chairman at MIT, once remarked: "There is always a time when the longer view could have been taken and a difficult crisis ahead foreseen and dealt with while a rational approach was still possible. How do we avoid such extremes?...Only with foresight—the central ethic of leadership—for so many bad decisions are made when there are no longer good choices."

Chances are we have all seen the results of actions taken without foresight, without examining likely consequences. Think of the relationships shattered by ill-considered words or undisciplined actions. Consider the wars fought and millions of lives lost because leaders never clearly counted the costs before the first bomb was dropped or the first soldier sent into battle. Much analysis of the recession of 2008 focuses on executives who foresaw only the enormous profits they would reap from the sloppy, often fraudulent mortgages they wrote, while ignoring the predictions of the near ruin their practices would bring to the whole economy.

Foresight is central to the moral life. Returning to a point made in the Introduction, each decision we make *reveals* our values and purpose in life, *tests* our commitment to our values and vision, and *shapes* the future. Each action we take casts a shadow forward. Each person and every servant leader has to make decisions and take action; these are not optional. David Young, an American Baptist pastor and author of *Servant Leadership for Church Renewal*, wrote: "Failure to act...when you still have the freedom to act, is unethical because you fail to act responsibly when the moment of opportunity is available. Leading is critical here. The responsibility is heavy because you must act before all the evidence is in."

Foresight like that of Francis is developed through listening and empathy, which deepen our understanding, meditation and reflection, and by keeping our vision always at the forefront. Jesus clearly advised us to grow in foresight and hinted at the consequences of acting without it:

> Not everyone who says to me, 'Lord, Lord,' will enter the kingdom of heaven, but only the one who does the will of my Father in heaven....
>
> Everyone then who hears these words of mine and acts on them will be like a wise man who built his house on rock. The rain fell, the floods came, and the winds blew and beat on that house, but it did not fall, because it had been founded on rock. And everyone who hears these words of mind and does not act on them will be like a foolish man who built his house on sand. The rain fell, and the floods came, and the winds blew and beat against that house, and it fell — and great was its fall! (Matthew 7:21-27)

After his conversion, Francis strove to put on the mind of Christ and act accordingly. No matter what happened to him — illness, rejection, abuse — his house was built on the rock of the Gospels. He had the foresight to know that, as the old hymn says:

No storm can shake my inmost calm
while to that Rock I'm clinging.
Since Love is Lord of heaven and earth
how can I keep from singing.

And, indeed, Francis did sing.

We grow in foresight as we develop the other key characteristics of a servant leader: listening, awareness, empathy, persuasion, and conceptualization. These qualities support us when we look down the road toward the end of our actions and the results of our decisions.

Learning Franciscan Foresight

• Looking Ahead by Assessing Now: Foresight is highly intuitive, but like Louis Pasteur said, "Chance favors the prepared mind." Various techniques have been utilized to help individuals and organizations look ahead and prepare for the future. One of these approaches is the SWOT analysis: S = strengths, W = weaknesses, O = opportunities, and T = threats. Picturing Francis using such a process requires some imagination. However, when we look at his writings and the stories about him, we can see that he had a firm grasp of the community's SWOT. Many online resources provide examples of doing an organizational SWOT analysis. Individuals may do one too. Doing a SWOT analysis provides a good opportunity to brainstorm, to open our consciousness to possibilities, and to see things in fresh ways that might challenge our status quo. Try to find a time and place in which you will not be interrupted. Perhaps begin with silent prayer, asking for the aid of your Advocate, the Holy Spirit. Here are the simple steps that you might use for a personal SWOT analysis:

○ **Strengths** are the qualities of character and positive attributes that may be built on for the common good and an abundant future. For each question, list as many responses as possible.

> What are the positive personal traits with which I have been blessed?
>
> What are my skills? Competencies? Work experiences?
>
> What is my education? What particular areas of knowledge do I have?
>
> What network of friends, colleagues, and family do I have? What are my communities of support?
>
> What is my vision, mission, or passion that gives me energy and direction?

○ **Weaknesses:** We all have limitations and undeveloped areas interiorly; these, too, influence our future.

> What negative attributes do I have (for example, quick temper, procrastination)?
>
> What are some skills or competencies that I have needed, but never developed?
>
> What education would prove useful to have when looking forward?
>
> Which networks of support do I need to develop?
>
> Do I have a clear sense of mission? If not, what have been the effects of that absence?

○ **Opportunities** are external events over which we have no control, but to which we can respond creatively and positively if we have given them some consideration beforehand.

When I look at developments in my learning and growth as a person, what opportunities might open up for me?

What relationships do I have that would help me explore new opportunities as a servant to the common good, to building the Reign of God?

Are there exciting trends in my field of expertise that will offer opportunities to expand my mission?

Do I have any inklings of God calling me to new challenges?

What are some "high-priority needs" in my community that I might be able to address to help others become freer, wiser, healthier, more autonomous, and more likely themselves to become servants?

○ **Threats** consist of external forces in life that oppose the achievement of our mission and stifle our work for a common good.

What obstacles challenge my mission? Funding? Lack of support? Shortage of will?

Are there any other organizations or communities that stand in opposition to my mission?

Are any of my weaknesses going to prevent me from moving effectively toward my vision?

○ Generate as many ideas and as much data as you can for each area. Then review everything—perhaps having taken a breather from it. Showing your SWOT to close friends might help you amplify some areas.

○ Taking this reflection further, you might want to use specific areas as the subject of prayer and meditation, trying to reach some fresh understanding and perhaps a plan of action. Call on the Holy Spirit to guide you.

- Tree of Possibilities: This exercise in foresight was originally designed to help young writers compose plots for stories. It is also an interesting and helpful way to examine possible consequences of courses of action. The idea is to build a tree of possibilities for some idea or action you wish to take. Using a large piece of paper will give you plenty of room to grow your "tree." The result will look a bit like a family tree:

  ○ In the center at the top of your paper (like the star on top of your Christmas tree), write down an idea you want to explore or action you wish to take; for example, I want to begin a volunteer agency of advocates for the elderly in my community.

  ○ Next, create three branches on the next level. Write three possible actions or consequences that flow from this desire to create a group of advocates; for example, talk to Pastor Ellen, search for agencies doing this already, fit it somehow into my busy schedule.

  ○ Create the next "branches" on the tree: Under each of the three actions or consequences, write down three possible actions or consequences; for example, under search for agencies: contact Dorothy, call the Aging and Disability Department, check with medical center chaplain. (You may have more than three ideas; add them too, but make sure you have at least three per idea.)

  ○ Next, you should have nine actions or consequences at level three. Before you expand your list, you may need to do the calling or make the contacts. But, you guessed it: Now write three actions or consequences under each one of the nine ideas.

- ○ Keep expanding your "tree" as far as proves useful.

- ○ Once you have worked this much on your tree, you can begin taking action.

- Toward the end of his life, Francis wrote his "Testament." In effect, he wanted to re-emphasize the most important values and inspiration that would guide the friars when he was no longer living among them. Write your testament, telling the future generation what is most important in order to live abundantly in service to a common good.

Final Reflections

Hindsight is 20/20. Foresight is not. Even so, foresight can mature in us if we consistently reflect on and pray over the flow of life: the past as part of the present, leading to the future. Servant leaders take up the task of foresight because they want every decision to have positive consequences for a common good. Servant leaders keenly sense the relationship between present action and future consequences. They think like grandparents, or even great-grandparents, who pose the question: How is what I am doing now going to affect my grandchildren and great-grandchildren?

Offer this prayer, which ended Francis' Letter to the Entire Order, asking for foresight, guidance, and solid direction toward the Reign of God:

Almighty, eternal, just and merciful God,
give us miserable ones
the grace to do for You alone
what we know you want us to do
and always to desire what pleases You.
Inwardly cleansed,
interiorly enlightened

and inflamed by the fire of the Holy Spirit
may we be able to follow
in the footprints of Your beloved Son,
our Lord Jesus Christ,
and, by Your grace alone,
may we make our way to You,
Most High,
Who live and rule
in perfect Trinity and simple Unity
and are glorified
God almighty,
forever and ever.
Amen.

(*FA:TS* 120-121)

8

Being the Good Steward

In the Porziuncola woodlands one day, in the burning dog-days, a cricket breaks the empty noonday silence with its song. The brothers, who had risen before dawn to recite the hours, are asleep. So now in the merciless heat the praises to the Lord are sung by the cricket....

Francis, motionless among the still oaks, listens, enraptured.... He is delighted by this little creature from which comes such vibrant harmony....

Francis calls, "My sister cricket, come to me."

And the cricket comes immediately from a hiding place in a fig tree into his hand.

Francis says, "Sing, my sister cricket, and praise your Creator with a joyful song."

And the cricket begins to sing again.... He speaks to her about his thoughts, his desires, his dreams. He speaks of God who is splendor and harmony. He talks of light and shadow, of beautiful life and silent death.

Finally he lifts his hand and the cricket returns to its tree. Eight days pass and the cricket does not move from that tree. When Francis leaves his cell, she is ready to fly to his hand, to sing or be silent according to his command. At the end of that time Francis says to his companions, "Let us give our sister cricket leave to go, for it has made us sufficiently happy now. We do not want our flesh to glory vainly over things of this kind."

So the cricket takes flight beyond the tree and is lost in the sky. It never returns. (Fortini, *Francis of Assisi*)

*S*uch wonderful stories of Francis' love of and harmony with God's creation abound. The stories of the wolf of Gubbio, the birds to whom he preached, and the earthworm crossing the path that he carried to safety inspire and amuse us. At the heart of all these stories is a central truth about Francis as a leader: We are sisters and brothers to animals and plants, water and soil, earth and sky.

In God's plan and Francis' spirituality, we do not own or control our sisters and brothers. As Psalm 24:1 proclaims, "The earth is the Lord's and all that is in it." To abuse, dominate, or denigrate any of God's creation—earth, animal, human—is an attempt to abuse, dominate, or denigrate what is the Creator's. Instead, we are called to live in peace and love with all "the earth," which "is the Lord's."

All of Creation is the Body of Christ. Theologian Sallie McFague says, "The body of Christ is not a body, but all the different, peculiar, particular bodies about us.... We do not use nature or other people as a means to an end—our union with God—but see each and every creature, every body, as intrinsically valuable in itself, in its specialness.... The model of the world as God's body encourages us to dare to love bodies and find them valuable and wonderful—just that and nothing more. The 'God part' will take care of itself if we can love and value the bodies." Christ has redeemed all of creation (Romans 8:22)—all the Body of Christ—and calls us to love and respect all parts of the Body.

Pope John Paul II declared Francis the patron of ecology. Of course, this is fitting. "Ecology" comes from two Greek words: *oikos*, meaning "household," and *logos*, meaning "word" or "reason." The ecologist expresses the essential truths about the household—all of Creation. Ecology, at its heart, is caring for the earth. In his actions and words, Francis cared for the earth. He models good stewardship for all generations.

In *Stewardship: Choosing Service over Self-Interest*, Peter Block offers a description of stewardship in sync with Francis and the Bible: "Stewardship is to hold in trust the well-being of some larger entity—our organization, our community, the earth itself. To hold something of value in trust calls for placing service ahead of control.... Service is central to the idea of stewardship." Good stewards recognize that they are "earthen vessels" and their lives fleeting. They are called to serve a common good for generations to come by serving the Body of Christ now.

Franciscan poverty has its roots in stewardship. Francis understood that ownership seemed invariably to lead to selfishness and greed rather than service to a common good. Francis let the cricket fly away freely lest he and the friars begin to "glory vainly over things of this kind." He knew that even sister cricket should not be a possession.

For Francis and any follower of Christ, all of life is "the Lord's." Francis took the Gospel command to "sell everything and give to the poor" literally. He was not to possess anything because all things should be shared. The Later Rule of the order declares: "Let the brothers not make anything their own, neither house, nor place, nor anything at all. As pilgrims and strangers in this world, serving the Lord in poverty and humility, let them go seeking alms.... Wherever the brothers may be and meet one another, let them show that they are members of the same family" (*FA:TS* 103). Ownership cuts us off from one another. Franciscan poverty and stewardship made the friars "members of the same family"—all people and all creation.

Francis' love of the earth and its goodness invited him to rejoice in the cricket's song, and out of that love he served the good of all, especially those most in need. This story typifies Francis' stewardship of "things."

It happened once that a poor man met him on his return from Siena, when, because of an illness, he was wearing a short mantle over his habit. When his kind eye observed the man's misery, he said to his companion: "We must give back to this poor man his mantle, for it is his! For we accepted it on loan until we should happen upon someone poorer than we are." But his companion, seeing the need of his pious father, objected to this stubbornly, lest by providing for someone else, he neglect himself. But he said, "The great Almsgiver will accuse me of theft if I do not give what I have to someone in greater need." (*FA:TF* 589)

For stewards like Francis, all "goods" of earth are on loan from the Creator. "The great Almsgiver will accuse" us of theft when we do not serve those in greater need.

In one way or another, stewardship includes all of the other nine qualities of a Franciscan leader. Franciscan leader-stewards realize their interdependence with all humanity, all God's creatures, and the holy earth. They are also challenged by Franciscan poverty. Friar William Short in his book *Poverty and Joy* says, "It is the relinquishment of wealth, status and domination over others that the incarnation teaches Francis and Clare.... Following this example, living *sine proprio*, without anything of one's own, today implies the refusal to arrogate to one's self what belongs to all, because all belongs to the Creator. Everything is gift, nothing is 'property'. The gospel mandate to 'sell all and give to the poor', which Francis and Clare followed, far from being meaningless, is as urgent in our own day as it was in theirs."

So, Franciscan leaders hold God's creation in trust for a common good, not in ownership. They adhere to the American Indian belief that "We do not inherit the land from our ancestors, we borrow it from our children." Their love and care for Creation grows from their relationship with all their sisters and brothers: humans, animals, earth, wind, and sky.

Learning Franciscan Stewardship

• Franciscan leaders renew their commitment to being good stewards by regularly nurturing their wonder at and relationship with Creation. The Book of Wisdom says, "For it is wisdom who gave me unerring knowledge of what exists, to know the structure of the world and the activity of the elements" (7:17-18). Resolve to observe creation closest to home. Find a place outside to sit quietly or walk softly. Absorb the sounds all around you. Offer the Creator a response, and talk to the Creator about other ways of knowing the earth. You might respond to what you experience with "Praise God!" For instance, "Praise God through the swaying silver maple tree."

• As an examen of conscience, recall two ways in which you have cared for Creation over the last two days. Then think of two ways in which you could show more respect—be a better steward—for God's Creation.

• Francis treated all creatures as brothers and sisters, with gentleness and respect. Do your patterns of consumption in your home, at work, in your ministry reveal a gentle spirit toward Creation? Are you possessed by any of your possessions? Do you hold them in trust or hold them as owner?

• Read Mark 3:1-6. Pause and reflect: Would you treat your body and the body of the world differently if you believed them to be the very body of God? Resolve to add this image of God to your understanding of the relationship between God and Creation.

• Franciscan stewards know where their food comes from and honor and respect its growth and those who grow it. Tending a garden or even a houseplant connects us to Creation. If you have nothing green, start with caring for a houseplant;

start a window herb garden, join a community gardening co-op. Give your hands the gift of digging in the earth.

- 1 Peter 4:10-11 reads: "Like good stewards of the manifold grace of God, serve one another with whatever gift each of you has received. Whoever speaks must do so as one speaking the very words of God; whoever serves must do so with the strength that God supplies, so that God may be glorified in all things." The Franciscan leader understands that all is gift, and the gift she or he receives is used in God's glory. Reflect on this passage. Talk with God about the gifts you have been given and how you have employed them for God's glory.

- In periods of reflection, ponder Jesus' words: "Wherever your treasure is, that is where your heart will be too" (Luke 12:34). Where is your treasure?

- Go back to any of the passages about or from Francis at the start of this chapter. Use it for meditation on your own stewardship.

- If you stood before God today and had to give an account of your stewardship, would God tell you, "Well done, good and faithful servant," or something more severe?

- If you wish to do a more thorough and formal evaluation of your stewardship, many online resources can lead you through a home sustainability audit or an organizational/ company audit. One useful home audit may be found at: http://oregonstate.edu/sustainability/sustainability-audits.

- Finally, pray with Francis' Canticle of the Creatures. Ponder its meaning for you.

Final Reflections

Good stewardship is a key responsibility of Franciscan leaders whether they are parents, government officials, community members, friends, or executives. But what sustains good stewardship is joy in the community of all Creation praising the Creator. Francis' Canticle of the Creatures sings God's praises and reminds us that God's love is in all and for all time:

Most High, all-powerful, good Lord,
    Yours are the praises, the glory,
    and the honor, and all blessing,

To You alone, Most High, do they belong,
    and no human is worthy to mention Your name.

Praised be You, my Lord, with all Your creatures,
    especially Sir Brother Sun,
    Who is the day and through whom You give us light.

And he is beautiful and radiant with great splendor;
    and bears a likeness of You, Most High One.

Praised be You, my Lord,
    through Sister Moon and the stars,
    in heaven You formed them
    clear and precious and beautiful.

Praised be You, my Lord, through Brother Wind,
    and through the air, cloudy and serene,
    and every kind of weather,
    through whom You give sustenance to Your creatures.

Praised be You, my Lord, through Sister Water,
    who is very useful and humble and precious and chaste.

Praised be You, my Lord, through Brother Fire,
    through whom You light the night,
    and he is beautiful and playful and robust and strong.

Praised be You, my Lord, through our Sister Mother Earth,
who sustains and governs us,
and who produces various fruit
with colored flowers and herbs....

Praise and bless my Lord and give Him thanks
and serve Him with great humility.

9

A Resource for Growth

*F*rancis, who wouldn't even claim his ragged robe as his own, gave what he could — namely, himself — to anyone in need. Bonaventure relates this story:

> While he was secluded in a cell on Mount La Verna, one of his companions was yearning with great desire to have something of the Lord's words commented on and written with his own hand. He believed that by this means he would be set free from — or at least could bear more easily — a serious temptation which oppressed him, not in the flesh but in the spirit. Though growing weary with such a desire, he was in a state of inner anxiety because, overcome with embarrassment, he did not dare to disclose it to the venerable father. But what man did not tell him, the Spirit revealed. He ordered that brother to bring him paper and ink. And he wrote down with his own hand the Praises of the Lord according to the brother's desire, and, at the end, a blessing for him, saying: "Take this paper for yourself and keep it carefully until your dying day." The brother took the gift he so much desired and his temptation disappeared immediately. The letter was preserved and, since later it worked wonders, it became a witness to the virtues of Francis. (*FA:TF* 618)

Francis the careful listener and empathetic soul constantly served the friars, the servants of the poor. He was their central resource for growth in the life of the Gospels. So he shared his wisdom, his love, his example, so that they could be ministers in turn.

Furthermore, knowing that he would not be able to serve the friars forever, he gave them a Rule that held mutual service at its core:

> Let each one confidently make known his need to another that the other might discover what is needed and minister to him. Let each one love and care for his brother as a mother loves and cares for her son in those matters in which God has given him the grace. Let the one who does not eat not judge the one who does. (*FA:TS* 71)

In another section of the Rule, he adds:

> If the brothers, wherever they may be, cannot observe this life, let them have recourse to their minister as soon as they can, making this known to him. Let the minister, on his part, endeavor to provide for them as he would wish to be provided for him were he in a similar position.
>
> Let no one be called "prior," but let everyone in general be called a lesser brother. Let one wash the feet of the other. (*FA:TS* 68)

Francis led the friars not by power over them, but as one who serves, one who sought their good and shared the resources they needed. This is what Franciscan leaders do.

Harvard ethicist Joseph L. Badaracco, Jr. could be talking about Francis' way of leading when he says that the most effective leaders "move patiently, carefully, and incrementally. They do what is right—for their organizations, for the people around them, and for themselves—inconspicuously and without casualties.... I have come to call these people *quiet leaders* because their modesty and restraint are in large measure responsible for their impressive achievements" (*Leading Quietly*). Surely the people of Assisi knew Francis, but the small deeds of service that helped individual friars grow in the life of the Gospels were done quietly, simply, modestly—the type of leadership needed.

Franciscan leadership is often like that: quiet, simple, modest acts that influence others to grow in the life of Christ. These actions are not done for applause and recognition, but for the good of others. This is the type of leadership that Francis exerted and which many people have come to understand as exemplary, effective leadership. Albert Schweitzer, winner of the Nobel Peace Prize for his ministry among African lepers, wrote in his autobiography:

> Of all the will toward the ideal in mankind only a small part can manifest itself in public action. All the rest of this force must be content with small and obscure deeds. The sum of these, however, is a thousand times stronger than the acts of those who receive wide public recognition. The latter, compared to the former, are like the foam on the waves of a deep ocean. (Quoted in *Leading Quietly*)

The power of Franciscan leadership is most often felt in the force of "small and obscure deeds" and, over the centuries has become a deep ocean of leadership for a common good.

Francis quietly led the friars, and of course was a source of good for all the people with whom he lived. Three years before he died, Francis organized the Christmas celebration with the people at Greccio. He likely never thought that the manger scene would become a mainstay of Christmas observance all over the world. He was doing what Franciscan quiet leaders do, gathering people to be formed by the Gospel:

> He had a manger prepared,
> hay carried in and an ox and ass led to the spot.
> The brethren are summoned,
> the people arrive,
> the forest amplifies with their cries,

and the venerable night is rendered
brilliant and solemn
by a multitude of bright lights
and by resonant and harmonious hymns of praise.
The man of God stands before the manger,
filled with piety,
bathed in tears, and overcome with joy.
A solemn Mass is celebrated over the manger,
with Francis, a levite of Christ, chanting the holy
Gospel.
Then he preaches to the people standing around
him
About the birth of the poor King,
whom, whenever he means to call him,
he called in his tender love,
the Babe from Bethlehem....
For Francis's example,
when considered by the world,
is capable of arousing
the hearts of those who are sluggish in the faith of
Christ.

(*FA:TF* 610)

Francis' "example" aroused the hearts of the people. The resource of the Christmas crib that he gave us continues to empower people to remember the birth of Jesus as a powerful and concrete event.

Franciscan leaders offer others the resources they need to become servants themselves. Francis showed the ministers how to serve the friars and showed the people at Greccio how to celebrate Christ's birth. Jesus commissioned the disciples to heal the sick, raise the dead, drive out demons, and preach the Gospel. He even declared, "Very truly, I tell you, the one who believes in me will also do the works I do and, in fact, will do greater works than these" (John 14:12). In short, they led others to live as Christ through their example, resources, and support.

Becoming Resources for Growth

• G. K. Chesterton said of Francis: "He honoured all men; that is, he not only loved but respected them all. What gave him his extraordinary personal power was this: that from the Pope to the beggar, from the sultan of Syria in his pavilion to the ragged robbers crawling out of the wood, there was never a man who looked into those brown burning eyes without being certain that Francis Bernardone was really interested in *him*; in his own inner individual life from the cradle to the grave; that he himself was being valued and taken seriously" (*St. Francis of Assisi*). Make a list of people who are active in your life. Ponder Chesterton's words, asking yourself: When these people look into my eyes, do they see interest, valuing, and serious care? How am I a resource for their growth in the Gospels? In their work? In their personal life?

• Franciscan leaders need not and usually don't have all the answers to help people. Indeed, sometimes questions might be the best approach, inviting the Spirit to be with you in the discernment. Ask: How might I be of help? What do you need to deal with this? What resources do I have that might be of use to you? Are there ways for me to help you discern other possibilities?

• One principle of Franciscan leadership is that those in positions of authority work for those who "work for" them. Ken Blanchard, in *Leading at a Higher Level*, says, "Their role is to help people achieve their goals. They constantly try to find out what their people need to perform well and live according to the vision." Recall Francis' instructions to the friars to make their needs known to the ministers. In turn, Franciscan leaders then respond, and often what might be "needed" is simply a return phone call, a short conversation, a visit to someone on behalf of the one needing help, or something else seemingly simple. Many times what will support a person is an affirming comment, a kind greeting, or an inquiry about how things are going. Ask yourself: How do I really work for those who work for/with me?

• Wise leaders like Francis realize that they depend on the know-how, gifts, and wisdom of the other people in their organization, family, school, or community to accomplish their mission. Thus, they figure out ways to include others in decisions. Max De Pree, former CEO of Herman Miller, Inc., wrote: "Everyone comes with certain gifts—but not the same gifts. True participation and enlightened leadership allow these gifts to be expressed in different ways and at different times. For the CEO to vote on the kind of drill press to buy would be foolish. For the drill press operator (who should be voting on the kind of tool to use) to vote on whether to declare a stock split would be equally foolish" (*Leadership is an Art*). Give De Pree's comment some serious thought, and then challenge yourself to explore new ways to effectively involve and empower people in decision making.

• In becoming a totally volunteer organization, the U.S. military had to rethink its approach to and training for leadership. In point of fact, employees of companies, members of organizations, and even adult family members are actually volunteers. Jack Lowe, Jr. of TDIndustries concludes: "Your best employees have the talent and ability to leave your company and find work elsewhere if they want to. So you should lead them the way you lead volunteers" (quoted in Keith, *The Case for Servant Leadership*). Do you agree with Lowe? How would someone lead if she or he believed that all others in the community or business or family were volunteers?

Final Reflections

Franciscan leaders support, affirm, and resource those with whom they live and work. Such leadership is about love: fostering the good of others. To repeat, James A. Autry, former president of the Meredith Corporation, declared, "Leadership is...about caring for people and being a useful resource for people.... Leadership requires love." Jesus and Francis gave us the perfect examples of loving leadership.

One of the most poignant examples of Francis as loving leader is the letter he wrote to Brother Leo, his faithful companion for many years. It challenges us to be leaders characterized by generous self-giving. It was written toward the end of Francis' life, after he had received the stigmata. The wear and tear on the letter suggests that Leo most likely carried it with him constantly for the rest of his life. We can imagine the outpouring of love that came through Francis' pen as it was held in hands marked by the wounds of Christ:

> Brother Leo, health and peace from Brother Francis!
>
> I am speaking, my son, in this way—as a mother would—because I am putting everything we once said on the road in this brief message and advice. If, afterwards, you need to come to me for counsel, I advise you thus: In whatever way it seems better to you to please the Lord God and to follow His footprint and poverty, do it with the blessing of the Lord God and my obedience. And if you need and want to come to me for the sake of your soul or for some consolation, Leo, come. (*FA:TS* 122)

This is what Franciscan leaders may still say: "If you need and want to come to me for the sake of your soul," the support of your mission, or "for some consolation," come.

10
Building Community

*T*he final characteristic of Franciscan leaders is that they are community builders. They seek to create circles of support, inspiration, and service. Acknowledging that everyone is due respect and has valuable gifts to offer, Franciscan leaders see themselves as part of and responsible to the community. Thomas of Celano tells that Francis sent the friars out to preach in various regions of Europe. But he sorely missed them and wanted to see them and hear of their progress:

> Coming together in one place,
> they celebrate with great joy on seeing their
> devoted shepherd,
> and they are amazed that
> the same desire to come together moved all of
> them in this way.
> They report the good things
> which the merciful Lord was doing for them,
> and if they had been somewhat negligent and
> ungrateful,
> they humbly ask and carefully accept
> correction and punishment from the holy father.

They always acted in this way when they came to him, and they did not hide from him the least of their thoughts or even impulses of their souls.... For a pure spirit so possessed that whole first school of blessed Francis that, though they knew how to carry out things that were useful, holy and just, they were completely ignorant of how to rejoice over them with vanity. The blessed father, embracing his sons with unbounded love, began to open up to them his proposal and to show them what the Lord had revealed to him. (*FA:TS* 209)

Francis keenly rejoiced in gathering the friars. Particularly in the early years when the community was just forming, such gatherings played an important role in focusing their energies and providing support for one another.

The fraternal love that Francis encouraged and the friars embraced continued even when Francis was not present:

> What a great flame of charity burned in the new disciples of Christ!
> What great love of devout company flourished in them!
> When they all gathered somewhere
> or met each other on the road (which frequently happened),
> in that place a shoot of spiritual love sprang up,
> scattering over all love the seeds of real delight.
> What more can I say?
> There were
> chaste embraces, delightful affection, a holy kiss, sweet conversation,
> modest laughter, joyful looks, a clear eye,
> a supple spirit, a peaceable tongue, a mild answer,
> a single purpose, prompt obedience, and untiring hands.
> (*FA:TS* 217-218)

Thomas of Celano describes here what community is about: single purpose, joyful looks, sweet conversation, delightful affection. All of these define Franciscan leaders who build community.

Francis' commitment to building community among the friars extended to directions in the Rule: "Wherever the brothers may be and meet one another, let them show that they are members of the same family. Let each one confidently make known his need to the other, for if a mother loves and cares for her son according to the flesh, how much more diligently must someone love and care for his brother according to the Spirit!" (*FA:TS* 103). Of course, as with any family, the friars argued, gossiped, and grumbled, but Francis did what he could with God's grace to gather them in love and a single purpose, and to make sure that each one's needs were met. This is Franciscan leadership for the long-haul.

Francis' admonitions and example regarding community building have their roots, like all of his teachings, in the Gospels. Sayings from the Bible sprinkled his sentences. In his final moments of life, he had a brother read John's Gospel to him. He would have heard the story of Jesus washing the feet of the community and telling the disciples to do likewise for one another. He would have heard Jesus tell the people, "Just as I have loved you, you also should love one another. By this everyone will know that you are my disciples, if you have love for one another" (13:34-35). Franciscan leaders try to do likewise, because building community is not only commanded by the Gospel, it also ensures that the mission of the school, or hospital, or business will continue into the future when the "leader" or founder is gone.

Learning How Franciscans Build Community

• The early Christian communities gave witness to the type of community that Jesus and Francis would wish for: "The whole group of those who believed were of one heart and soul.... There was not a needy person among them" (Acts

4:32-34). Reflect on all the communities to which you belong: family, congregations, organizations, businesses, schools. Then ask yourself if each community is "of one heart and soul" and if there are "needy persons" among the community. What might be your role in addressing any disunity or needs among the people?

• One company that steadily makes the list of great places to work is Southwest Airlines. They work constantly at building community among their people. Community depends on healthy, helping relationships among people. Too often those in leadership positions do not get to know the folks they work with. So, managers at Southwest are taught "GTHOOYO," which means "Get the Heck Out of Your Office." This leadership style is also known as Management by Walking Around, meeting and acknowledging and learning from the employees who are doing the work at all levels of the company's operations. Francis would certainly applaud this practice for leaders. Whatever your position in the various communities to which you belong, reflect on your own practice of Management by Walking Around. How well do you know the people you work or worship with? Do you have any habits that separate or distance you from others?

• Meetings are one of the common venues for building community; anyone in leadership certainly spends considerable time in them. Write a list of upcoming meetings. Then, reflect—perhaps in writing—about how you can employ the following suggestions to make sure these are times of community building. Here are some criteria of meetings that build community:

  ○ *Are all parties invited to participate in forming the agenda?* Francis encouraged the friars to state their needs. What they revealed helped set his agenda. So, invite those who will be attending to contribute to the agenda. This is a great way to develop new leaders and get other people more invested in the work of your community. Then invite three or four folks together to finalize it. Send out the agenda at least a week before the meeting. This tells people that you respect their input and hope that they will come prepared to help. Remember, it's everyone's meeting, so everyone needs to buy in to the agenda. You can ask for feedback on the agenda before you begin the actual meeting.

o *Do people leave feeling they have been listened to?* To form community, people need to feel respected. Listening to each other carefully is a sign of respect. Ask yourself: Does everyone have a chance to participate. Do I invite participation? If you are leading the meeting, be gentle, but firm: people respect a meeting that is run well and remember all too clearly the meetings that were dominated by a particular personality or point of view. If someone goes off the agenda or speaks too long, draw them back in. If the group seems to want to go beyond the established time limit for an issue, ask for agreement from all members. Take the group's pulse on the matter with a statement and question such as: "We've already used our allotted time for this issue. Would everyone like to continue on the topic for another ten minutes, or shall we go on to the next item on the agenda?"

o *Is the discussion focused on issues or problem-solving, not personalities?* Summarize what you hear. Wrap up each agenda item by summarizing any conclusions out loud. Then move on when no one objects or everyone agrees. While harmonious relationships help build community, so does accomplishing important work of the community.

○ *Are the deliberations inclusive: that is, are all in attendance invited to contribute?* If a usually quiet person speaks, show your appreciation. Try to draw everyone in. Give positive reinforcement. Try rotating chairing responsibility. Use open-ended questions that urge people to say more than "yes" or "no."

○ Do participants own the decisions and feel accountable for results? Occasionally survey the group to ask for their views on both the process of the meetings and the actionable results.

○ Are there times for celebration? In Francis' description of that gathering of friars, celebration played an important part: It incorporated "sweet conversation," "joyful looks," and "modest laughter." When people are breaking bread together, they are relaxed and more open to revelation. Celebrate accomplishments, but also have informal time before and after the meeting for people to talk and socialize. Remember, sometimes "the meeting after the meeting" is where people get attached to the group — and also find their best ideas to bring to the next meeting!

○ Do the meetings focus on the vision or mission of the group? Some groups begin with a reading of the organization's mission or goal. Other groups start with a prayer or reflection, giving people time to recollect themselves.

• Celebrate. The early Christian communities celebrated together. Celebration held them together in the face of oppression. We celebrate birthdays and anniversaries to support and encourage people. Company picnics or banquets gather employees to say "thank you." More than just being "nice," celebrations are a key to building community. Returning to the Southwest Airlines example, the company has a whole unit that plans and implements celebrations for employees, vendors, and customers. Franciscan leaders nourish and facilitate celebrations. What do you think? Are there ways in which you can make celebrations more a part of your community? Family? Business?

Final Reflections

Communities that we used to rely on have gone into sharp decline. Most churches are hemorrhaging membership. Clubs and civic organizations show dwindling numbers even as they try to support projects in the community. Too easy use of lay-offs to make the bottom line look better has destroyed the notion of company loyalty. Technology has made it possible for people to work at home while seldom actually meeting anyone face to face. Social networking provides a false sense of creating personal relationships and genuine community.

Even so, the desire—the need—for real relationships and supportive community still urges us to seek ways of making these connections. People are healthier, wiser, freer, and more fully alive in community. Francis knew that, and the creation of community is a challenge that all Franciscan leaders encounter.

Even as he was dying, Francis continued to bring the brothers together to celebrate and support one another by singing "The Canticle of the Creatures," which he wrote when he was blind and infirm. Francis even composed the melody to the song. The story goes that Francis enjoyed the song so much that he sought the services of Brother Pacifico and several other friars. They were to sing and teach the Canticle wherever they preached. In his biography of Francis, Fortini says, "They were to sing like minstrels, who formed a ring in city piazzas.... One of the friars was first to preach a sermon, then all of them would sing Francis's song. Afterwards, the one who had preached was to turn to the people and say, 'We are the jongleurs of God and the only reward we want is to see you lead a truly penitent life.'" As Francis' death drew near and his pain increased, he asked the friars to "sing his song of joy for him to gain the strength to endure every pain" (*Francis of Assisi*). Francis was a leader to the end, showing the community how to strengthen him during his excruciating illness and one another during the pain of his loss. To the end, he was a builder of community.

Epilogue

*G*od told Francis, "Go and repair my house which, as you see, is all being destroyed" (*FA:TF* 536). We have the same invitation to repair the Church, our local community, and the *oikos*, our home, the whole of creation.

The forces of destruction have timeless names: greed, anger, selfishness, ignorance, carelessness. Francis saw these forces at work in his time; they are still at work in ours. The forces of good are also timeless: love, faith, hope, wisdom, generosity, courage, kindness. Francis exemplified these virtues in his time; with the grace of God, we can be examples for ours.

Leadership is not an option for human beings; we all influence others to act. If we are to build God's house — the reign of God here and now — then we embrace servant leadership that:

- with empathy and awareness, listens to people's pleas and their wisdom
- has a vision of God's reign and the foresight to make decisions now that will guide us to it
- builds a community of service and resources all members to reach fullness of life
- knows that we hold all creation in trust for the future

In the footsteps of Jesus, Francis was just such a servant leader. We can be also.

Right now, we live in a climate of suspicion and cynicism about leaders, so it is no wonder that people look toward servant leaders wherever they are found, and embrace Pope Francis, who has taken Saint Francis as his model. In his first letter to the world, *The Gospel of Joy*, Francis echoes his namesake when he says:

> I beg the Lord to grant us more politicians who are genuinely disturbed by the state of society, the people, the lives of the poor! It is vital that government leaders and financial leaders take heed and broaden their horizons, working to ensure that all citizens have dignified work, education and healthcare. Why not turn to God and ask him to inspire their plans? I am firmly convinced that openness to the transcendent can bring about a new political and economic mindset which would help to break down the wall of separation between the economy and the common good of society.
>
> Economy, as the very word indicates, should be the art of achieving a fitting management of our common home [*oikos*], which is the world as a whole.

Pope Francis models what he preaches. He is modeling the servant leadership of Jesus and Francis of Assisi.

Robert Greenleaf described servant leadership and articulated how it transforms people who then transform organizations. But servant leadership is as old as the Gospel and is rooted in God's Word: "In everything do to others as you would have them do to you; for this is the law and the prophets" (Matthew 7:12).

People from various faith traditions admire and love Francis of Assisi because he lived this Golden Rule. He loved inclusively, passionately, generously, and wisely. The ten characteristics of a servant leader are all qualities of the self-giving love that forms the heart of servant leaders.

Leading like Francis builds God's house. There can be no better life and noble calling. And so we end with the prayer written in the spirit of Francis that asks for the gifts of Franciscan servant leadership:

Make me an instrument of your peace.
Where there is hatred, let me sow love;
where there is injury, pardon;
where there is doubt, faith;
where there is despair, hope;
where there is darkness, light;
where there is sadness, joy.
O, Divine Master, grant that I
may not so much seek to be consoled as to console;
to be understood as to understand;
to be loved as to love.
For it is in giving that we receive;
it is in pardoning that we are pardoned;
it is in dying that we are born to eternal life.

References and Further Reading

Armstrong, Regis J., J. A. Wayne Hellmann, and William J. Short, Eds. *Francis of Assisi: Early Documents: Vol. 1 – The Saint, Vol. 2 – The Founder, Vol. 3 – The Prophet.* New York: New City Press, 1999, 2000, 2001.

Autry, James. *The Servant Leader: How to Build a Creative Team, Develop Great Morale, and Improve Bottom-Line Performance.* New York: Prima, 2001.

Badaracco, Joseph L., Jr. *Leading Quietly: An Unorthodox Guide to Doing the Right Thing.* Boston: Harvard Business School Press, 2002.

Blanchard, Ken. *Leading at a Higher Level.* Upper Saddle River, NJ: Pearson/Prentice Hall, 2007.

Blanchard, Ken and Phil Hodges. *The Servant Leader: Transforming Your Heart, Head, Hands, and Habits.* Nashville, TN: J. Countryman, 2003.

Block, Peter. *Stewardship: Choosing Service over Self-Interest.* San Francisco: Berrett Koehler, 1993.

Bodo, Murray. *Tales of St. Francis.* Cincinnati: St. Anthony Messenger Press, 1988.

Boff, Leonardo. *Saint Francis: A Model for Human Liberation.* New York: Crossroad, 1990.

Chesterton, G. K. *St. Francis of Assisi.* Garden City, NY: Doubleday Image Books, 1924.

De Pree, Max. *Leadership is an Art.* New York: Dell Publishing, 1989.

Fortini, Arnaldo. *Francis of Assisi.* New York: Seabury, 1981.

Greenleaf, Robert K. *Servant Leadership: A Journey into the Nature of Legitimate Power and Greatness.* New York: Paulist, 1977.

Hunter, James C. *The Servant: A Simple Story about the True Essence of Leadership.* New York: Prima, 1998.

Johnston, William, ed. *The Cloud of Unknowing and The Book of Privy Counseling.* New York: Doubleday, 1973.

Keith, Kent. M. *The Case for Servant Leadership.* Westfield, IN: Greenleaf Center for Servant Leadership, 2008.

Koch, Carl J. *Journalkeeping.* Notre Dame, IN: Sorin Books, 2003.

McFague, Sallie. *The Body of God: An Ecological Theology.* Minneapolis: Fortress Press, 1993.

Phelps, Owen. *The Catholic Vision for Leading Like Jesus.* Huntington, IN: Our Sunday Visitor, 2009.

Short, William J. *Poverty and Joy: The Franciscan Tradition.* Maryknoll, NY: Orbis, 2004.

Spears, Larry, ed. *Insights on Leadership: Service, Stewardship, Spirit, and Servant Leadership.* New York: Wiley, 1998.

Steindl-Rast, David. *Gratefulness, the Heart of Prayer: An Approach to Life in Fullness.* New York: Paulist Press, 1984.

Wheatley, Margaret J. *Leadership and the New Science.* Berrett-Koehler, 1999.

Website:

www.greenleaf.org – The Greenleaf Center

NEW CITY PRESS
of the Focolare
Hyde Park, New York

New City Press is one of more than 20 publishing houses sponsored by the Focolare, a movement founded by Chiara Lubich to help bring about the realization of Jesus' prayer: "That all may be one" (John 17:21). In view of that goal, New City Press publishes books and resources that enrich the lives of people and help all to strive toward the unity of the entire human family. We are a member of the Association of Catholic Publishers.

Further Reading—Books from New City Press

Books by Regis J. Armstrong, William J. Short & J. A. Wayne Hellmann (eds.)

Francis of Assisi: Early Documents - The Saint
                                978-1-56548-110-7 $49.95
Francis of Assisi: Early Documents - The Founder
                                978-1-56548-112-1 $39.95
Francis of Assisi: Early Documents - The Prophet
                                978-1-56548-114-5 $49.95
Francis of Assisi: Early Documents - Index
                                978-1-56548-171-8 $15.95

Other titles of interest:

Gospel Joy - Pope Francis and the New Evangelization,
Dennis J. Billy, C.Ss.R.   978-1-56548-566-2 $11.95
Day by Day with Saint Francis - 365 Meditations,
Gianluigi Pasquale, OFM Cap. (ed.)   978-1-56548-394-1 $24.95

Periodicals

Living City Magazine,
www.livingcitymagazine.com